THE DARK SIDE OF THE MOON

THE DARK SIDE OF THE MOON

THE MAKING OF THE PINK FLOYD MASTERPIECE

JOHN HARRIS

 DA CAPO PRESS   A MEMBER OF THE PERSEUS BOOKS GROUP

Library of Congress Cataloging-in-Publication Data

Harris, John, 1969–
    The dark side of the moon : the making of the Pink Floyd masterpiece / John Harris.—1st Da Capo Press ed.
        p. cm.
    Includes bibliographical references (p.   ) and index.
    ISBN-13: 978-0-306-81342-9 (hardcover : alk. paper)
    ISBN-10: 0-306-81342-4 (hardcover : alk. paper)   1. Pink Floyd (Musical group). Dark side of the moon.
2. Rock music—History and criticism.   I. Title.
    ML421.P6H37 2005
    782.42166'092—dc22

    2005014735

First Da Capo Press edition 2005
Published by Da Capo Press
A Member of the Perseus Books Group
www.dacapopress.com

Da Capo Press books are available at special discounts for bulk purchases in the U.S. by corporations, institutions, and other organizations. For more information, please contact the Special Markets Department at the Perseus Books Group, 11 Cambridge Center, Cambridge, MA 02142, or call (800) 255-1514 or (617) 252-5298, or e-mail *special.markets@perseusbooks.com*.

Design by Cooley Design Lab
Text set in Adobe Garamond/Display set in Gill Sans

1 2 3 4 5 6 7 8 9 — 08 07 06 05

For Hywel, who was right.

CONTENTS

"I don't miss Dave, to be honest with you," said Roger Waters, his voice crackling down a very temperamental transatlantic phone line. "Not at all. I don't think we have enough in common for it to be worth either of our whiles to attempt to rekindle anything. But it would be good if one could conduct business with less enmity. Less enmity is always a good thing."

He was speaking from Compass Point Studios, the unspeakably luxurious recording facility in the Bahamas whose guestbook was filled with the signatures of musicians of a certain age and wealth bracket: the Rolling Stones, Paul McCartney, Eric Clapton, Joe Cocker. Waters was temporarily resident there to pass final judgment on the kind of invention to which that generation of musicians was becoming newly acquainted: a 5.1 surround-sound remix, one of those innovations whereby the music industry could persuade millions of people to once again buy records they already owned.

No matter that Pink Floyd's *The Dark Side of the Moon* had already been polished up to mark its twentieth anniversary in 1993; having been remixed afresh, it was about to be packaged up in newly designed artwork, and re-released yet again. Its "30th Anniversary SACD Edition" would appear two months later, buoyed by an outpouring of nostalgia, and the quoting of statistics that had long been part of its authors' legend.

The fact that they had the ring of cliché mattered little; *Dark Side*'s commercial achievements were still mind-boggling. In the three decades since it appeared, the album had amassed worldwide sales of around thirty million. In its first run on the U.S. album charts, it clocked up no less than 724 weeks. In the band's home country, it was estimated that one in five households owned a copy; in a global context, as the British magazine *Q* once claimed, with so many copies of *Dark Side* sold, it was "virtually impossible that a moment went by without it being played somewhere on the planet."

That afternoon at Compass Point, Waters devoted a couple of hours to musing on the record's creation, and its seemingly eternal afterlife. "I have a suspicion that part of the reason it's still there is that successive generations of adolescents seem to want to go out and buy *The Dark Side of the Moon* at about the same time that the hormones start coursing around the veins and they start wanting to rebel against the status quo," he said. When asked what the record said to each crop of new converts, he scarcely missed a beat: "I think it says, 'It's OK to engage in the difficult task of discovering your own identity. And it's OK to think things out for yourself.'"

As he explained, *Dark Side* had all kinds of themes: death, insanity, wealth, poverty, war, peace, and much more besides. The record was also streaked with elements of autobiography, alluding to Waters's upbringing, the death of his father in World War II, and the fate that befell Syd Barrett, the sometime creative chief of Pink Floyd who had succumbed to mental illness and left his shell-shocked colleagues in 1968. What tied it all togeth-er, Waters said, was the idea that dysfunction, madness, and conflict might be reduced when people rediscovered the one truly elemental characteristic they had in common: "the potential that human beings have for recogniz-ing each other's humanity and responding to it, with empathy rather than antipathy."

In that context, there was no little irony about the terms in which he described the album's place in Pink Floyd's progress. In Waters's view, the aforementioned statistics concealed the Faustian story of the band finally achieving their ambitions, and thus beginning the long process of their dis-solution. "We clung together for many years after that—mainly through fear of what might lie beyond, and also a reluctance to kill the golden goose," he said. "But after that, there was never the same unity of purpose. It slowly became less and less pleasant to work with each other, and more and more of a vehicle for my ideas, and less and less to do with anyone else, so it became less and less tenable." In the words of Rick Wright, at the time *Dark Side* was created, "it felt like the whole band were working together. It was a creative time. We were all very *open.*" Thereafter, Waters became so commanding that the possibility of any such joint endeavor was progressively closed down.

Naturally, you could hear some of this in the music. The band's collective personality on *Dark Side* is warmly understated—a quality embodied in the gentle vocal blend of Wright and David Gilmour—and most of the sentiments expressed are intentionally universal: within the sea of personal pronouns in Waters's lyrics, none occurs as often as "you." From 1975's *Wish You Were Here* onward, however, Waters recurrently vented the very specific concerns of an increasingly troubled rock star. Underlining the change, as of Pink Floyd's next album, 1977's rather bilious *Animals,* Gilmour's vocals were nudged to one side, while Waters's unmistakable mewl became the band's signature.

All this reached its conclusion on *The Wall,* the 1979 song-cycle-cum-grand-confessional-and-concert spectacular that, in financial terms at least, achieved feats that even *Dark Side* hadn't managed. Arguably the greatest achievement on *Dark Side* is "Us and Them," a lament for the human race's eternal tendency to divide itself into warring factions. By the time of this new project, which Waters still believes is of a piece with the band's best work ("I think *The Wall* is as good as *The Dark Side of the Moon*—I think those are the two great records we made together"), Pink Floyd's music suggested one such example: Roger Waters versus the rest of the world.

Where *Dark Side* oozed a touching generosity of spirit, *The Wall* was bitterly misanthropic. Though the former combined its melancholy with hints of redemptive optimism, the latter seemed unremittingly bleak. And if the 1973 model of Pink Floyd had been a genuinely collective endeavor, by 1979, Gilmour, Wright, and Nick Mason were very much supporting players (indeed, Wright had been fired during *The Wall* sessions). All this reached a peak with 1983's *The Final Cut*—according to its credits, "A requiem for the post-war dream by Roger Waters, performed by Pink

Floyd." In its wake, Waters expressed the opinion that the band was "a spent force creatively," announced his exit, and assumed that the story had drawn to a close. At least one account of this period claims that Waters's parting shot to his colleagues was "You fuckers—you'll never get it together."

Much to Waters's surprise—and against the backdrop of a great deal of legal tussling—Gilmour eventually decided to prolong the band's life, creating his own de facto solo record, 1987's *A Momentary Lapse of Reason*, and then enlisting Mason and Wright—the latter as a hired hand rather than an equal partner—for a world tour that found the group earning record-breaking receipts and settling into the life of a stadium attraction. In 1994, they released their second post-Waters album, *The Division Bell*, and commenced a vast world tour partly sponsored by Volkswagen. "I see no reason to apologize for wanting to make music and earn money," said Gilmour. "That's what we do. We always were intent on achieving success and everything that goes with it."

Waters, watching from afar, could not quite believe that Pink Floyd now denoted a group whose live presentations were built around an eight-piece band, and whose latest album featured songs credited to Gilmour and his wife, an English journalist and writer named Polly Samson. "I was slightly angry that they managed to get away with it," he said in 2004. "I was bemused and a bit disappointed that the Great Unwashed couldn't tell the fucking difference…. Well, actually they can. I'm being unkind. There are a huge number of people who can tell the difference, but there were also a large number of people who couldn't. But when the second album came out … well, it had got totally Spinal Tap by then. Lyrics written by the new wife. Well, they were! I mean, give me a fucking break! Come *on!* And what a nerve: to call *that* Pink Floyd. It was an awful record."

So it was that Gilmour and Waters had arrived at the impasse that defined their relations in the early twenty-first century. The upshot in 2003 was clear enough: a record partly based on the desirability of greater human understanding was being promoted by two men who had not spoken for at least fifteen years.

The week that Waters arrived at Compass Point, David Gilmour—long known to his friends and associates as Dave, before insisting on his full Christian name at some point during the 1990s—was at his home in the English county of Sussex, apparently embroiled in distanced negotiations with his old friend and colleague. "We're in second-hand contact," he explained. "James Guthrie, our engineer, is remixing the album. Roger listens to it and I listen to it, and we both give our comments and have our little battles over how we think it should be through someone else. I've just had no contact with Roger since '87 or something. He doesn't seem to want any. And that's fine."

Gilmour responded to questions about *The Dark Side of the Moon* with his customary reserve, couching a great deal of what he said in a businesslike kind of modesty. The record might have been elevated into the company of the nine or ten albums that go some way to defining what rock music is (or perhaps used to be): *Highway 61 Revisited, Revolver, Pet Sounds, The Band, Led Zeppelin IV,* et al. It undoubtedly continued to send thousands of listeners into absolute raptures. Yet at times, Gilmour still sounded surprised by what had happened. When asked about his memory of first appreciating the album in its entirety, he said this: "I don't think any of us were in any doubt that we were moving in the right direction, and what we were getting to was something brilliant—and it was going to be more critically and commercially successful than anything we'd done before.... I knew that we were moving up a gear, but no one can anticipate the sales and chart longevity of that nature."

Every now and again, he could allow himself a laugh at the kind of absurdity that comes with such vast success. There was a gorgeous irony, for example, in the fact that Roger Waters had intended *Dark Side*'s lyrics to be unmistakably direct and simple, only to see all kinds of erroneous interpretations heaped on them—not least the absurd theory, circulated in the mid-1990s, that *Dark Side* had been created as a secret soundtrack to *The Wizard of Oz.* "I think Roger had got sick of people reading everything wrongly," said Gilmour. "He was always talking about demystifying ourselves in those days. And *The Dark Side of the Moon* was meant to do that. It was meant to be simple and direct. And when the letters started pouring in saying, 'This means this, and this means that,' it was 'Oh *God.*' But as the years go by, you realize that you're stuck with it. And thirty years later you get *The Wizard of Oz* coming along to stun you. Someone once showed me how that worked, or didn't work. How did I feel? *Weary.*"

As had become all but obligatory in his interviews, Gilmour also reflected on the creative chemistry that had once defined his relationship with Waters and fired the creation of Pink Floyd's best music. "What we miss of Roger," he said in 1994, "is his drive, his focus, his lyrical brilliance—many things. But I don't think any of us would say that *music* was one of the main ones … he's not a great musician." Nine years on, he was sticking to much the same script: "I had a much better sense of musicality than he did. I could certainly sing in tune much better [laughs]. So it did work very well."

Over in the Bahamas, Roger Waters had angrily pre-empted any such idea. "That's *crap,*" he said. "There's no question that Dave needs a vehicle to bring out the best of his guitar playing. And he is a great guitar player. But the idea, which he's tried to propagate over the years, that he's somehow more musical than I am, is absolute fucking nonsense. It's an absurd notion, but people seem quite happy to believe it."

All that apart, and presumably to Waters's continuing annoyance, Gilmour was still the effective custodian of the Pink Floyd brand name. His last performance under that banner had taken place on October 29, 1994, in the echo-laden surroundings of London's Earl's Court Arena; poetically—and in brazen denial of its chief architect's continued absence—the show had been built around a rendition of *The Dark Side of the Moon.*

Now, when asked about the prospects of any further Pink Floyd records or performances, he sounded jadedly noncommittal. "At the moment, it's something so far down my list of priorities that I don't really think about it. I don't have a good answer for you on that. I would rather do an album myself at some point, and get on with other things for the time being. Would I rule it out? *Mmmm.* Not a hundred percent. One never knows when one's vanity is going to take one."

In June 2005, there came news so unlikely as to seem downright surreal. After a period of estrangement lasting two decades, Roger Waters and David Gilmour announced that they would both participate in a Pink Floyd reunion at the London Live 8 concert, aimed at pressuring the leaders of the world's wealthiest nations into a new accord on Africa. "Like most people, I want to do everything I can to persuade the G8 leaders to make huge commitments to the relief of poverty and increased aid to the third world," read a statement issued by Gilmour (who, according to subsequent reports, had initially been extremely reluctant to take part). "Any squabbles Roger and the band have had in the past are so petty in this context, and if re-forming for this concert will help focus attention, then it's got to be worthwhile."

Waters, meanwhile, issued a communique that sounded a slightly more gonzo note than his reputation as one of rock music's intellectual sophisticates might have suggested. "It's great to be asked to help Bob [Geldof] raise public awareness on the issues of third world debt and poverty," he said. "The cynics will scoff—screw 'em! Also, to be given the opportunity to put the band back together, even if it's only for a few numbers, is a big bonus." His return, however temporary, seemed to provide retrospective confirmation that the Pink Floyd who had authored *A Momentary Lapse of Reason* and *The Division Bell* had not been the genuine article, though the Gilmour statement came with a slightly different spin: "Roger Waters will join Pink Floyd to perform at Live 8," ran the headline on the official Pink

Floyd website.

The group's subsequent performance at London's Hyde Park—"Breathe/Breathe Reprise," "Money," "Wish You Were Here," and "Comfortably Numb"—was a delight, imbued with a poise and grace that only enhanced the music's impact. Moreover, the few words spoken to the crowd served to underline both the unlikeliness of the reunion and where it stood in the band's labyrinthine history. "It's actually quite emotional, standing up here with these three guys after all these years," said Waters. "Anyway, we're doing this for everyone who's not here, particularly, of course, for Syd."

Inevitably, the show sent interest in the Floyd's music skyrocketing; according to one British newspaper, the day after Live 8 saw sales of the career anthology *Echoes* rising by 1,343 percent. Talk of a lasting rapprochement, however, was quickly squashed (for all its wonders, Gilmour said the experience was as awkward as "sleeping with your ex-wife"). For the time being, Pink Floyd's creative history thus remains sealed, long since hardened by hindsight into a picture of peaks, troughs, and qualified successes.

To take a few examples at random, 1967's *The Piper at the Gates of Dawn* is fondly loved by a devoted fan-cult, and couched in the semi-tragic terms of an artistic adventure that was ended far too soon. *Ummagumma* (1969) is treasured by only hardened disciples; *Wish You Were Here* often seems as worshipped as *The Dark Side of the Moon*. *Animals* and *Meddle* (1971) are the kind of records that those who position themselves a little higher than the average record buyer habitually claim to be underrated and overlooked—and when *The Wall* enters any discussion, its champions often shout so passionately that any opposing view is all but drowned out.

By way of underlining Waters's view of their history, the two albums that Gilmour piloted in his absence are rarely mentioned these days. The accepted view of their merits is that they represented "Floyd-lite," an invention that worked very well as a means of announcing mega-grossing world tours, but hardly stood up to the band's best work. That said, the idea that most of Pink Floyd's brilliance chiefly resided in the mind of Roger Waters has been rather offset by the underwhelming solo career that began with 1984's *The Pros and Cons of Hitchhiking*—proof, despite the occasional glimmer of brilliance, that he too is destined to toil in the slipstream of the music he created in the 1970s.

The record with the most inescapable legacy is, of course, *The Dark Side of the Moon*—an album whose reputation is only bolstered by the fascinating story of its creation. Far from being created in the cosseted environs of the recording studio, it was a record that lived in the outside world way before it was put to tape: played, over six months, to audiences in American cities, English towns, European theaters, and Japanese arenas, while it was edited, augmented, and honed by a group who well knew they were on to something.

Perhaps most interestingly, it is a record populated by ghosts—most notably, that of Syd Barrett. In seeking to address the subject of madness, and to question whether the alleged lunacy of particular individuals might be down to the warped mindset of the supposedly sane, Roger Waters was undoubtedly going back to one of the most traumatic chapters in Pink Floyd's history—when their leader and chief songwriter, propelled by his prodigious drug intake, had split from a group who seemed to have very little chance of surviving his departure. For four years after Barrett's exit, through such albums as *A Saucerful of Secrets, Atom Heart Mother,* and *Meddle,* they had never quite escaped his shadow; there is something particularly fascinating about the fact that the album that allowed them to finally break free was partly inspired by his fate.

All that aside, *Dark Side* is the setting for some compellingly brilliant music. There are few records that contain as many shiver-inducing elements: the instant at which the opening chaos of "Speak to Me" suddenly snaps into the languorous calm of "Breathe"; just about every second of "The Great Gig in the Sky" and "Us and Them"; the six minutes that begins with "Brain Damage" and climaxes so spectacularly with "Eclipse."

Nor are there many examples of an album being defined by a central concept that would be so enduring. Other groups have come up with song cycles based on ancient legend, the sunset of the British Empire, futuristic dystopias, and pinball-playing messiahs. Pink Floyd, to its eternal credit, opted to address themes that would, by definition, endure long after the record had been finished, and the band's bond had dissolved.

That *Dark Side* hastened that process only adds to the story's doomed romance. "With that record, Pink Floyd had fulfilled its dream," said Roger Waters, as the transatlantic static fizzed and he prepared to return to *Dark Side*'s new remix. "We'd kind of *done* it."

Over in England, David Gilmour had voiced much the same sentiments: if only on that one subject, he and his estranged partner seemed to be united. "After that sort of success, you have to look at it all and consider what it means to you, and what you're in it for: you hit that strange impasse where you're really not very certain of anything anymore. It's so fantastic, but at the same time, you start thinking, 'What on earth do we do *now?*'"

I

THE LUNATIC IS IN MY HEAD:
SYD BARRETT AND THE ORIGINS OF PINK FLOYD

On July 22, 1967, the four members of Pink Floyd were en route to the Scottish city of Aberdeen, the most northerly destination for most British musicians. The next night, they would call at Carlisle, Cumberland, where they would share the stage with two unpromisingly named groups called the Lemon Line and the Cobwebs. Such was the life of a freshly successful British rock group in the mid- to late 1960s: a seemingly endless trek around musty-smelling ballrooms, where the locals might be attracted by the promise of seeing the latest Hit Sensation, and musicians could be sure of being rewarded in cash. If London proved too far for a drive home, they and their associates would be billeted to a bed and breakfast: the nightmarish invention that the British came up with instead of the motel, whereby travelers could rest their heads in a house commanded by an ill-tempered landlady, and breakfast on such delicacies as lukewarm tea, soggy toast, and canned mushrooms.

If this aspect of Pink Floyd's life hardly suggested any kind of glamour, they could take heart from the fact that they were—for the moment at least—accredited pop stars. The week they arrived in Aberdeen, their second single had climbed to number six in the U.K. singles charts, nestling just below the Beatles' "All You Need Is Love" and Scott Mackenzie's "San Francisco (Be Sure to Wear Some Flowers in Your Hair)." As with their first effort, "Arnold Layne," "See Emily Play" was a perfect exemplar of the influences wafting into Britain from the American West Coast being rewired into a very English sense of fairy-tale innocence, an impression only furthered by the Old World elegance of its lyrics, established in the opening line: "Emily tries/But misunderstands …"

The single's success had been boosted by a run of appearances in the kind of magazines that treated their subject matter with a breathless superficiality—like *Disc and Music Echo*, a weekly that tended to portray musicians as short-lived items on an accelerated production line. The day Pink Floyd were in Aberdeen, it honored them with its cover, accompanied by a set of pen-portraits, doubtless bashed out in a matter of minutes.

Roger Waters, said the magazine, "likes to think he is a hard man, and

The Pink Floyd Sound, Stanhope Gardens, North London, 1965. Left to right: Rick Wright, Roger Waters, Nick Mason, guitarist Bob Klose, Syd Barrett. (Nick Mason's Archive)

in fact he can be very evil.... He only listens to pop music because he has to." Maintaining the sense of a kind of withering demystification, Nick Mason was accused of getting "a kick out of being nasty to people—he likes people to be frightened of him, because he is someone of whom you could never be frightened." Rick Wright, meanwhile, was "the musician of the group, and also very moody. He has written hundreds of songs that will never be heard because he thinks they are not worthy."

The most lengthy character sketch was given over to Syd Barrett. Pink Floyd's singer, guitarist, and chief songwriter was described as "the mystery man of the group—a gypsy at heart ... he loves music, painting and talking to people ... totally artistic ... believes in total freedom—he hates to impede or criticise others, and hates others to criticise others or impede him." Barrett, it was claimed, "doesn't care about money and isn't worried about the future."

If such words suggested a blithe kind of contentment, the reality of Barrett's life was rather different. His London home was shared with people reputed to be "messianic acid freaks," fond of introducing their acquaintances to LSD on the slightest pretext. Barrett's familiarity with the drug long predated his arrival in their company, but his housemates were hardly ideal company: by now, Barrett's acid use was beginning to manifest itself in chronic mood swings that could lead to either raging anger—and occasional violence—or spells of near catatonia.

Inevitably, all this was starting to have an impact on the group's working lives. Seven days after the Aberdeen show, Pink Floyd played at a huge London event grandly titled The International Love-In. Mere minutes before stage-time, Barrett had gone AWOL; an associate of the band eventually found him, "absolutely gaga, just totally switched off, sitting rigid, like a stone." Pushed onto the stage, Barrett remained pretty much silent, apart from the odd moment when he decided to pull flurries of discordant notes from his guitar. Though his three colleagues did their best to somehow cover up for him, it was clear that something was wrong: in the wake of the show, reports in the music press made mention of "nervous exhaustion."

Nonetheless, Pink Floyd's work-rate hardly slowed down. By September, they were in Scandinavia. Six weeks later, after another run of British shows, they took off for their first tour of the United States, during which Barrett's problems would worsen yet further. The most-documented episodes from this period are an appearance on *The Pat Boone Show* that saw Barrett reacting to his host's questions with a glassy-eyed stare and large-scale silence, and a three-minute spot on *American Bandstand* in which Barrett reacted to the instruction that he should mime to "See Emily Play" by keeping his mouth resolutely shut.

It is some token of the band's frenetic schedule that two days after they returned to the U.K., they were back on tour, this time in the company of Jimi Hendrix. "There was a bit of 'Syd'll pass out of it, it's only a phase,'" says Nick Mason. "And I think we were anxious to make Syd fit in with what we wanted, rather than giving all our efforts to seeing if we could make him better. We probably said, 'Oh well—let's try and keep working.'

"Even now," says Mason, "I'm astonished. How could we have been so blinkered, or so silly, or so stupid?"

When talking to those who once shared Barrett's company, one facet of his story becomes clear: rather than the astral, saucer-eyed waif of legend, he was initially a gregarious, enthusiastic presence. "He was a very friendly soul," says Nick Mason. "At my first meeting, I can remember him bounding up and saying, 'Hello, I'm Syd'—at a time when everyone else would have been cool, staring around the room in a rather studied way, rather than introducing themselves."

"Syd was good fun," says Peter Jenner, half of Pink Floyd's initial management team. "He and I would sit around and smoke dope, listen to records, talk about things. Sharp? Absolutely. I had no idea he was going to go loopy; there was no indication. I had enormous respect for him, to the point of being overwhelmed: he did these paintings, and he wrote all these songs, and he played the guitar … he was full of ideas."

Barrett was born Roger Keith Barrett on January 6, 1946, and raised in the English university city of Cambridge. His father, Dr. Arthur Barrett, was a hospital pathologist; his mother, Winifred, was a housewife, who shared with her husband a love of classical music, and a wish to encourage their children's creative side via regular family "music evenings." Dr. Barrett died when Syd was fifteen; by that point, he had given his youngest son (Syd had two brothers and two sisters) a guitar, and Syd had begun to make contact with like minds. By 1962, he was the guitarist with a Cambridge band—in thrall to the standard beat-group archetype of the day—called Geoff Mott and the Mottoes, whose rehearsals tended to take place in the front room of the Barrett family home. Among their circle of intimates was Roger Waters: two years older than Syd, but happy, for now, to leave the slippery art of musicianship to his younger friend. "Syd was a little ahead of me," says Waters. "I was very much on the periphery. I can remember designing posters for Geoff Mott and the Mottoes, quietly wanting to be a bit further towards the center of things."

Barrett's musical activities, along with a talent for painting that led him to enroll at Cambridge's College of Art and Technology, soon drew him to the city's young in-crowd: a coterie of late-adolescent bohemians who would gather at the Criterion, a shabby pub located in Cambridge's center. He and Waters were soon among the regulars, sharing the company of a guitarist and teenage language student named David Gilmour, and Storm Thorgeson and Aubrey Powell, whose immediate ambitions lay, slightly vaguely, in film and photography.

"The thing that really struck me about Syd was that he was a kind of *elfin* character," says Aubrey Powell. "He walked slightly on his tiptoes all the time, and he used to sort of spring along. He always had a wry smile on his face, as if he was laughing at the world somehow. And he was always something of a loner: you could be with a group of people and suddenly

Following pages:

(left) Barrett and Peter Jenner, caught mid-way through the recording of *The Piper at the Gates of Dawn.* "I had no idea he was going to go loopy," says Jenner. "There was no indication." (Nick Mason's Archive)

(right) Roger Waters and Syd Barrett at Stanhope Gardens. "Syd was a little ahead of me," says Waters. (Nick Mason's Archive)

Syd would be gone. He'd just evaporate, and then two days later he'd return. He was very much his own person.

"What I really liked about him was this weird attention to detail. One day I went into his room, and he said, 'Look at these.' There were these three dodecahedrons hanging from the ceiling, all immaculately made from balsa wood: absolutely perfectly done. They were big, too. And I remember thinking, 'God, the *patience* to do that …'"

In the view of outsiders, Cambridge has a strong self-contained identity, forever bound up with its university, founded in the thirteenth century and revered for both its academic excellence and the splendor of its buildings and gardens. Though it attracts thousands of tourists to the city, the university is also responsible for the divide that separates the population into Town and Gown. For most young people born and raised in Cambridge, the university is an irrelevant, strangely distant institution; far more important is the close proximity of London.

Back in the 1960s, Syd Barrett, Roger Waters, and their friends were a perfect case in point. By the summer of 1964, the crowd centered on the Criterion was fast dissipating: Barrett had taken a place at Camberwell Art School, located in the British capital's Southern sprawl, while Waters was readying himself for studying architecture at the Regent Street Polytechnic, right in the city's center. The latter took very little time to make the move that, back in Cambridge, had always eluded him: drawing on his circle of newfound London friends, he formed a group called Sigma 6 and appointed himself its lead guitar player.

Waters's colleagues included a bass player named Clive Metcalf, vocalists Keith and Sheila Noble—and a drummer and rhythm guitarist who numbered among Waters's fellow architecture students. So it was that Nick Mason and Rick Wright entered the picture, later to be joined—after Waters had been nudged from lead guitar to bass, Wright had decided to play keyboards, and the band's more peripheral members had been pushed out—by Syd Barrett. He advised his new band that, having already passed through such ill-advised names as the T-Set, the Megadeaths, and the Abdabs—they should call themselves the Pink Floyd Sound, in partial tribute to two of his favorite blues singers, Pink Anderson and Floyd Council.

The group played its first show in late 1965 and began moving along the musical trajectory that would define their first career chapter. Like most groups of their era, they were partial to beat-group standards like "Louie Louie" and "Roadrunner," but they would use such songs as bookends to extended passages when, led by Barrett, they would step away from three-chord orthodoxy and begin to improvise. It is not hard to draw a line between such flights of musical fancy and Barrett's drug habits. Certainly, though his colleagues were not nearly as quick to ingest illicit substances, it's a matter of record that by the time of the Pink Floyd Sound's first maneuvers, Barrett was well acquainted with both cannabis and LSD.

In the summer of 1966, Peter Jenner, then a young economics graduate, chanced upon a Pink Floyd Sound performance at the Marquee, the London club where the Who had cut their teeth. "I was very into the idea of the young, groovy avant-garde," he recalls. "And I thought this would be a young, groovy, avant-garde show. I got there and saw the Floyd, and I thought they were remarkable, because I couldn't work out where each noise was coming from. The Marquee had a stage that kind of stuck out, and I was endlessly walking around it, just trying to figure it out.

"They were playing these really lame old tunes, like 'Louie Louie' and all these hackneyed blues songs—not much of Syd's stuff. But in the middle, there were all these *weird* bits going on: what I subsequently discovered were one-chord jams. Instead of there being a blues solo, there was a *weird* solo. And I liked that. I couldn't work out where the noise was coming from: whether it was guitar, or organ, or what. I just thought, 'Christ, this is interesting.'"

By 1966, a close-knit crowd of Londoners was beginning to coalesce into what would become known as the Underground. They formed a network of young creative people, plugged into a variety of cultural currents: the thrilling sense of possibility embodied by the recent—and unprecedented—success of English rock groups, led by the Beatles and Stones; a burgeoning drug culture; a thawing of social strictures that would soon be embodied in the legalization of abortion and homosexuality; and an economic climate that had given rise to full employment. Of no less importance were a slew of influences taken from the United States: the Beats, Bob Dylan, and most importantly of all, the freshly born West Coast counterculture—news of which had freshly crossed the Atlantic.

Suitably inspired, those at the center of London's bohemian milieux were starting to set up their own equivalent. The first issue of a weekly countercultural newspaper, *International Times* (aka *IT*), would be published in October 1966. Soon after, a late-night weekly event called UFO began in the unlikely environs of an Irish-themed London establishment called the Blarney Club. Elsewhere, art galleries, bookshops, and musical events were adding to the sense of a slow-building cultural upsurge.

The philosophical threads that held it all together were as varied as its constituent elements, but the Underground was unquestionably characterized by a shared agenda. Whereas previous radical movements had focused on the wish for change enacted on a grand scale—this being Great Britain, social class remained integral to most critiques of society—the '60s generation placed a new emphasis on the freeing of the individual, who would be liberated, according to the Underground's louder voices, by embracing the kind of multi-colored hedonism that defined London's hipper social circles.

According to Richard Neville, the Australian émigré who contributed to London's counterculture by editing the magazine *Oz,* "The aim of the alternative culture was to shake up the existing situation, to break down barriers not only between sexes and races and God knows what else, and it was also to have a good time … to enlarge the element of fun that one had occasionally in one's own life and to make that more pervasive—not just for you but for everyone. I was quite keen to abolish this work/play distinction. There was something incredibly oppressed about the mass of grey people out there. I just thought that people on the whole looked unhappy: they seemed to be pinched and grey and silly and caught up with trivia, and I felt that what was going on in London would bring color into those grey cheeks and those grey bedrooms. With a bit of sexuality and exciting music and flowers … somehow the direction of society could be altered."

If Syd Barrett's lifestyle implicitly allied him with the Underground's thinking, Peter Jenner was closely tied to some of its most crucial players. Together with John "Hoppy" Hopkins, a co-founder of *International Times,* he had established a record label called DNA—and, thrilled by what he had seen at the Marquee, Jenner initially approached the Pink Floyd Sound with a view to releasing their records. Led by Roger Waters, they persuaded him to instead take on the role of manager. In partnership with his long-standing friend—and a sometime employee of British Airways—Andrew King, Jenner thus founded the grandly named Blackhill Enterprises and began to assist his new clients. His first move was inspired: suspecting that the Pink Floyd Sound lent them an unbecoming air of vaudevillian corni-ness, he convinced them to trade as The Pink Floyd.

Via Jenner's connections, the group were rapidly placed at the heart of the Underground. In September 1966, they played the first of several fundraising shows for the Notting Hill Free School—a countercultural edu-cational experiment in which Peter Jenner was integrally involved—which took place at the Tabernacle, a church hall in West London. The next month, they appeared at the launch party for *International Times.* Two days before Christmas, they were the headliners at the first night of UFO, inau-gurating a relationship whereby The Pink Floyd were the club's house band, soundtracking its perfumed murk with music that seemed custom-made for that purpose.

Indeed, The Pink Floyd's outward aesthetic seemed designed to achieve a perfect fit between the band and their new audience. As strait-laced cover

versions were supplanted by Syd Barrett originals, the wildly improvisational element of their show had been built up to the point that it begged the voguish word "psychedelic" (indeed, ads for the Free School shows were strap-lined with Dr. Timothy Leary's maxim "Turn on, tune in, drop out"). And inspired by what little they knew of cutting-edge rock shows in the United States, the group now played their shows on stages flooded with the projections from homemade lighting equipment.

The result, according to those who had followed their progress from the start, was little short of revelatory. "They'd start a song like 'Astronomy Domine,'" says Aubrey Powell, "and work themselves up into a frenzy, and then it would all die down, and there'd be these long, almost embarrassing moments: you really wouldn't know what was happening. Syd would be playing weird sounds—there were real moments of tension in there. Then suddenly they'd get back to the song, and it would be concluded. It was amazing what Syd was able to do. There was something very unsettling about it. It really wasn't like watching any other band."

Outwardly, Pink Floyd seemed to number among the Underground's aristocracy. Aside from Barrett, however, they cautiously kept their distance —happy to play the shows, but surprisingly indifferent to either the substances or beliefs that tended to go with them. "The gigs that we played thanks to all that were *great*," says Roger Waters. "It was tremendous fun— going on at the Tabernacle and playing 'Louie Louie' for fifteen minutes. There were some of Syd's early songs in there, but a lot of what we did then came from the length of time we were expected to be onstage: sometimes, we'd play three sets in a night.

"But I never really knew any of those people that well. And to this day, I still don't know exactly what a lot of that stuff was actually about. You'd hear the odd thing about revolution, but it was never terribly specific. I don't know … I read *International Times* a few times. But, you know— what was the Notting Hill Free School actually all about? What was it meant to *do?*"

"There's a great quote from that period: 'They were all stoned, and we were drunk,'" says Nick Mason. "I think the association with the Underground was certainly a Flag of Convenience. I think we'd all concede that. But as usual with these things, there was good stuff there, interwoven with an enormous amount of absolute guff. There were some good ideas, and some very forthright liberal views—but the period was full of an equal number of people with tarot cards and crystals. The number of love beads that one accumulated … I never really thought it was a good way of designing one's future."

In February 1967, The Pink Floyd signed a contract with EMI, receiving an advance of £5,000 ($3,500). Their first single, released on March 11, had been recorded early in the new year under the supervision of Joe Boyd, the émigré American who was responsible for the musical aspects of UFO.

"Arnold Layne," the embodiment of a pop-minded economy that lay in polar opposition to the band's approach to performance, nonetheless managed to fill its three minutes with the sense that its authors were pushing their music into uncharted territory. The combination of Barrett's droning, distracted vocal, the song's subtle denial of a strict verse/chorus structure, and its subject matter—the lifestyle of a kleptomaniac transvestite, placed at the center of a very English picaresque—lent it the sense of the pop form being very cleverly subverted. When it crept onto the charts, sitting alongside singles by the Monkees, the Turtles, and the Dave Clark Five, the point was made explicit.

In the meantime, the group was the subject of a flurry of press attention, focused chiefly on the single's subject matter ("Meet the Pinky Kinkies!" ran one headline) and the allegedly mold-breaking nature of their shows. "The Pink Floyd offer a total show consisting of 700 watts of amplification, weird droning music (largely improvised) and lighting and slide projections using melting oil paints," said *Disc and Music Echo*. "On stage, the Floyd themselves become completely lost in their music and they aim

Following pages:

The Pink Floyd at UFO, 1967. "There was something very unsettling about it. It really wasn't like watching any other band." (Redferns/Adam Ritchie)

to absorb the minds of their audience too, which isn't easy with the usual cool atmospheres around London."

Crowds in the British capital, however, were soon proving to be the

least of their worries. With "Arnold Layne"'s muted success—it eventually rose to 21 in the U.K. singles chart, despite being excised from radio playlists on account of its risqué lyrics—Pink Floyd were inducted onto the circuit of regional British ballrooms that would define much of their lives for the next six months. Here, the group's pushing of the musical envelope counted for nothing: though the habitués of UFO and the Tabernacle might have thrilled to the band's extended experiments, outside London, people expected an altogether more orthodox kind of entertainment—music to dance to, and the simple pleasure of hearing the same hits that had recently blared from their radios.

"The industry was fundamentally different back then," says Peter Jenner. "Basically, you made your money gigging. That was your job: being a band meant you did six gigs a week—or if you were lucky nine, with double headers at the weekend. It was all about getting in the van, going off with your gear, and doing a gig. And then you would do a record—maybe if you did well, you did a single. And if you were lucky, that was a hit, and your fee went up."

"We'd do anything; we'd go anywhere," says Roger Waters. "You'd get in the van and look forward to the fifty quid. And it was hard work. I can remember a run of gigs that started in Douglas, on the Isle Of Man, and then went on to Norfolk, and the next day we were playing Elgin in Scotland. That is *a lot*. They could be vicious gigs, too: balconies that overlooked the stage, and people dropping pints of beer on us. And, of course, they'd all want to hear the hits. We often refused to play them."

"The one that really sticks in my mind is the Queen's Hall in Barnstaple: an old-fashioned ballroom that would have pop bands on," says Peter Jenner. "This place had a balcony around the top—and people *were* pouring beer on them. We needed the money, but there was a real conflict between the market they were playing into—a Top Twenty market—and what the band were playing: this really avant-garde stuff. We got the same problems every time they went out of London. It was all right when they were in the colleges: everyone would turn up with bells around their necks, carrying incense. But when you went elsewhere, it was difficult for them. They got a very hard time."

For now, the group's momentum was maintained, though the pressures of the band's schedule, exacerbated by his drug use, were beginning to exact their toll on Syd Barrett. In March 1967, they entered the hallowed environs of EMI's Abbey Road studios to work on their first album, *The Piper at the Gates of Dawn.* According to the terms of their contract, they were to work with a staff producer named Norman Smith, whose résumé at least contained one implicit recommendation: he had been chief engineer on every Beatles album up to *Rubber Soul.* Thanks chiefly to Barrett, however, his relationship with his new charges quickly proved to be rather fraught. "It was sheer hell," he later recalled. "There are no pleasant memories. I always left with a headache. Syd was undisciplined: he would never sing the same thing twice. Trying to talk to him was like talking to a brick wall, because his face was so expressionless … he was a child in many ways: up one minute, down the next."

For all Smith's trials, in Peter Jenner's estimation, he pulled off a commendable artistic feat: teasing out Barrett's sense of pop aesthetics from the instrumental tangle that defined Pink Floyd's performances. "What he did," says Jenner, "was to say, 'Well, you've written these jolly good pop songs— so let's have those, and some weird instrumental breaks.' So instead of being blues songs with weird instrumental breaks, it became pop songs with weird instrumental breaks."

Notice of the abiding idea was served by the opening track, "Astronomy Domine": from Barrett's supremely sinister opening growl of guitar, it is obvious that havoc is about to be played with the period's standard musical norms, but the song's exploratory, improvisational core is bookended by passages that betray both a tight sense of musical control, and an intuitive grasp of the melodic demands of pop. Even "Interstellar Overdrive," the instrumental mission-statement that found the spirit of their live shows being poured onto tape, is ultimately a showcase for the group's ability, having let loose chaos, to purposefully rein it back in. For all the lysergic abandon that takes root inside its first minute—punctuated by the kind of musical tension that Aubrey Powell found so compelling in the band's live shows—its central riff is the essence of both control and streamlined strength: certainly, when it gloriously re-enters the picture after eight and a half minutes, one gets a sense of the band single-mindedly returning to earth.

Piper's other most notable aspect was Barrett's lyrics. Whereas the music betrayed both power and sophistication, his words were recurrently founded in the fragile simplicity of childhood, often so innocently expressed that one cannot help but arrive at a crude explanation for Barrett's breakdown. How, it might be asked, could the kind of mind that came up with "The Gnome" ("Look at the sky, look at the river—isn't it good?"), or the rose-tinted memoir "Matilda Mother"—a loving remembrance of Winifred Barrett reading her son fairy tales—adapt to the hard demands of adulthood, let alone the pressures that arrive in the wake of commercial success? Rock music, even then, was only partly founded on talent and creativity; if a musician was to survive, he or she also needed wiliness, resilience, and determination: in short, a keen sense of ambition.

"Syd was a real hippie in a lot of respects," says Aubrey Powell. "If he had a guitar, and he could play some tunes, and sing some of his wonderful bits of poetry, and somebody could supply him with a nice space where he could play his Bo Diddley albums, that was enough. Even when he was earning money, Syd wasn't living extravagantly. He was quite happy to live in a flat with no furniture in it. He was a real bohemian in that sense. I never felt he was pop star material; he wasn't made for it."

The Piper at the Gates of Dawn was preceded by "See Emily Play," which thrust Pink Floyd into dizzying territory, climbing to number 6 on the British singles charts, and confirming the necessity of endlessly touring the country so as to prolong their success. By the time of its release, however, Syd Barrett was beginning to fall apart. "He became steadily more remote," says Peter Jenner. "He was hard to talk to. From being occasionally withdrawn, he got very *strange*. And his life became more and more his own life until we hardly saw him. That was when I really began to worry that there was something going seriously awry."

Most of the songs on *Piper* had been written during a concerted burst of creativity in late 1966 and early 1967, when Barrett was living in an apartment on Earlham Street in central London. In the recollection of his roommate, the group's lighting technician Peter Wynne-Wilson, "Those were halcyon days. He'd sit around with copious amounts of hash and grass and write these incredible songs. There's no doubt they were crafted very carefully and deliberately."

By April 1967, Barrett had shifted his base of operations to 101 Cromwell Road, an address in the Earl's Court area of West London. Among the residents was one Brian "Scotty" Scott, remembered by one Pink Floyd associate as "one of the original acid-in-the-reservoir, change-the-face-of-the-world missionaries." For Barrett, the upshot of such company was clear enough. "He seemed to be on acid every day," says Peter Jenner. "We heard he was getting it in his tea every morning." This, it was safe to say, was hardly the ideal lifestyle for someone whose sensibilities were proving ever-more fragile, but for the moment, neither the band nor their associates saw fit to intervene.

"Everything was coming at us from all directions," says Jenner. "In the (right) Syd Barrett at Abbey Road, spring 1967. "He wasn't pop star material; he wasn't made for it."

(opposite) Barrett, late 1967. "He seemed to be on acid every day. We heard he was getting it in his tea every morning."

(Nick Mason's Archive)

early days, when Syd was at Earlham Street, I'd just pop round there quite often and see him. As they became bigger, he moved into his own social scene. We saw less of him; he became more distant. We realized there was something strange going on in Cromwell Road, but I didn't know the people who were there. And I never really felt it was my job to find out. It was only when it became clear that there was a problem with gigging—with *work.* … In those days, it was really uncool—*man*—to pry into someone's life."

When the group and their associates attempted to deal with Barrett's predicament, they initially did so in the context of a quintessentially 1960s invention known as anti-psychiatry, one of the many strands of thought beloved of the upper echelons of the Underground. Relative to the other credos of the period, it was a neat fit: just as Underground insiders like Richard Neville believed that the key to social change lay with the moral and emotional liberation of the individual, so anti-psychiatry held that the shortcomings of twentieth-century civilization were reflected in isolated cases of supposed mental breakdown. The key pioneer of all this was a Scottish doctor named R. D. Laing, born in 1927, but sufficiently radical in his outlook to be co-opted into the Underground by his younger admirers.

Laing was fleetingly involved in the Notting Hill Free School, became a regular presence at Underground events, and was decisively tied into the mood of 1967 by that year's publication of a polemic, drawn from his lectures, entitled *The Politics of Experience*. Schizophrenia, the book claimed, arose from a rational desire

Abbey Road, 1967. "Everything was coming at us from all directions." (Redferns/Andrew Whittuck)

to opt out of impossible circumstances: "The experience and behaviour that gets labelled schizophrenic is a special strategy that a person invents in order to live in a unlivable situation." Moreover, the supposed schizophrenic might actually be capable of greater insights and achievements than the allegedly sane: in Laing's view, asking whether the condition was wholly due to a deficiency on the part of the sufferer was "rather like supposing that a man doing a handstand on a bicycle on a tightrope 100 feet up with no safety net is suffering from an inability to stand on his own two feet. We may well ask why these people have to be, often brilliantly, so devious, so elusive, so adept at making themselves so unremittingly incomprehensible." Underlying all this was the belief that society so squashed individual potential that mental dislocation was inevitable. "The ordinary person," Laing wrote, "is a shrivelled, desiccated fragment of what a person can be."

"There were a whole team of them who all believed it was rather good to be mad, and it was the rest of us who were making less sense," remembers Roger Waters. "And it may be that there is something to be said for the idea that people who we claim to be mad might see things that the rest of us don't, and their experience can illuminate life for us. He seemed to be thinking that insanity might be a very subjective idea; that perhaps madness might give people some kind of greater insight. In Syd's case, you could say that it was his potential for decline into schizophrenia that gave him the talent to express mildly untouchable things. But I confess that I feel that a lot less now than I may have done then."

"With Syd's very clear mental problems," says Peter Jenner, "there was a sense of, 'Well, is it our fault or his? Who's actually mad: him or the rest of us? Is the madman speaking truth?' For someone like me, who was quite young and pretentious and intellectual and read too many books, it was very hard to cope with. We knew something was a bit weird, but on the other hand, the Floyd's whole experience had been a bit weird. We were out there on the edge, so what was wrong with Syd being a bit out there on the edge? At what point does being original and new and different become loony? It seemed impossible to say. It's a continuum."

On one occasion, Barrett's colleagues arranged for him to meet Laing, only for Syd to decide at the last moment that he was unwilling to go through with it. "He wouldn't get out of the car," says Roger Waters, who accompanied Barrett to Laing's house. "And I'm not sure that was necessarily a bad thing. Laing was a mad old cunt by then. [Pause] Actually, 'cunt' is a bit strong. But he was drinking a lot."

Contrary to the fashionable thinking of the time—and in keeping with his distanced relationship with the Underground—Waters claims to have held fast to a conventional diagnosis of Barrett's problems. "Syd was a schizophrenic," he says. "It was pretty clear to me that that was what was the matter with him. But not everybody would accept that. I had ties with Syd's family going back a fair way, and I can remember telephoning one of Syd's brothers and telling him he had to come and get Syd, because he was in a terrible mess, and he needed help. And the three of us sat there, and in effect, Syd did a fairly convincing impression of sanity. And his brother said, 'Well, Roger says Syd's ill, but that's not the way it seems to me.'

"There was eventually a lot of argy-bargy with his family, and a lot of stuff about whose fault it was," says Waters. "His mother blamed me entirely for Syd's illness. I was supposed, I think, to have taken him off to the fleshpots of London and destroyed his brain with drugs. And the fact is, I never had anything to do with drug-taking. Certainly not with Syd, although he did indulge in lot of acid, which given the fact that he was an incipient schizophrenic was obviously the worst possible thing in the world for him. But mothers have favorite sons—and if something goes wrong, they have to find someone to blame."

Barrett's decline took place against the backdrop of frantic activity: the aforementioned U.S. tour, a run of British shows with the Jimi Hendrix Experience and the Nice, and attempts to record a new single, so as to capitalize on the success of both "See Emily Play" and *The Piper at the Gates of Dawn*. The fact that Barrett was able to honor the vast majority of his commitments seems faintly miraculous, although his behavior was leading to snowballing tension within the group. While Waters, Mason, and Wright would attempt to found the band's shows on at least some sense of structure, Barrett was prone to perpetrating musical anarchy, regularly detuning his guitar, and frequently proving reluctant to sing. For at least one show on the Hendrix tour, he could not even be persuaded to take the stage: so it was that David O'List, the Nice's guitarist, was cajoled into temporarily taking his place.

Barrett and Waters en route to Denmark in September 1967, when the latter was declining fast. "Syd's mother blamed me entirely for his illness," says Waters. (Nick Mason's Archive)

"We were irritated," says Nick Mason. "There was tendency to tut: a lot of 'Oh God.' And to some extent, we ignored it. That's the way I remember it: there wouldn't have been a big row in the dressing room. There was never any confrontation: it was very much, 'Let's avoid confrontation at all costs—for God's sake, let's try and pretend everything's all right. Let's not have a crisis. Maybe things will be all right if we just keep them going.' I think that's a peculiarly English thing anyway. But we didn't have those sort of skills in terms of [pause] human resources.

"On any given night, we had no idea what was going to happen. And it wasn't like every gig, or every song, being a disaster. I don't remember being onstage thinking, 'Here we go again.' Each time, it was a surprise."

In the recording studio, the impossibility of Barrett's position was increasingly evident. By way of a new single, he came up with "Apples and Oranges": in Roger Waters's view, "a fucking good song … destroyed by the production." In fact, it amounted to a loose-ended sketch that might conceivably have been honed into shape had its author not been in such a fragile state. The band's public certainly thought as much: though EMI was desperately hoping for a third hit, "Apples and Oranges" stiffed.

The run of sessions that produced that song also gave rise to three other Barrett-authored tracks, all of which attested to his decline. On "Jugband Blues," a song that teetered on the brink of collapse before being suddenly and inexplicably invaded by a Salvation Army band, he came close to expressing a chronic sense of self-alienation ("I'm not here ... And I'm wondering who could be writing this song"). "Scream Thy Last Scream," on which Barrett was accompanied by a speeded-up, inescapably irritating backing vocal, was eventually all but subsumed—for some reason—by a cacophony of audience noise. Perhaps most telling of all was a song called "Vegetable Man." If its lyrics superficially suggested a self-deprecating joke, it also betrayed a palpable sense of self-loathing, only accentuated by the churning, discordant music that made up its backing track.

On all four songs, the sense of inspired exploration that had been the hallmark of *The Piper at the Gates* had evaporated. Now, it seemed, Pink Floyd was simply tumbling into chaos.

By the end of 1967, Pink Floyd (the "The" would continue to crop up on posters and handbills until mid–1969, though its use was evidently on the wane) was at an unenviable career juncture. It was clear that Barrett's role was untenable; and yet the group's management was adamant that a future without his creative input was inconceivable. The one Roger Waters composition released thus far was "Take Up Thy Stethoscope and Walk," a musical makeweight that amounted to *Piper's* one glaring flaw; Rick Wright had contributed "Paintbox," as the B-side of "Apples and Oranges"—the breezy tale of a night on the town that was so lacking in any of the group's customary experimentalism that it skirted dangerously close to the dread category of Easy Listening.

To Peter Jenner and Andrew King, all this amounted to clear evidence that Barrett had somehow to be kept in the band. Waters, however, was adamant that he had to leave. "Roger was the leader of the 'Syd Must Go' faction," says Peter Jenner. "He was saying, 'We can't work with this guy anymore. It's impossible for us to go to a gig and have him turn up, or not turn up, and not give us a set list—it's making us look like prats.' He was out there on the frontline, whereas I was back in the office being intellectual about it. But he was aware that they were killing their career by doing these gigs with Syd, because they were turning off the punters. It was a complete mess. And I think the worst thing was the demand for another record, when there were no songs coming from Syd. It was, 'What the fuck are we going to do?' But the Syd faction—myself and Andrew—had no confidence in any of them writing without him."

By way of a compromise, it was suggested that the group should recruit a second guitarist, leaving Barrett to appear with the group when he was in sufficiently good shape, and to continue to write the group's songs. They thus made renewed contact with an old acquaintance from their days in Cambridge, David Gilmour, then making frustratingly little headway in a London-based trio called Bullitt. He accepted the offer of a new job, he later recalled, largely thanks to the prospect of "fame and the girls." On the former count, at least, he did not get off to the most promising start. By the time of the announcement of his recruitment in the music press, the group's stock had so fallen that the story was not exactly headline news: the *NME* gave it one small paragraph, and spelled the new member's surname "Gilmur."

In January 1968, the five-man incarnation of Pink Floyd played four shows, in Birmingham, the coastal resort of Weston-Super-Mare, and the Sussex towns of Lewes and Hastings. Aubrey Powell clearly recalls seeing at least one of those shows, and quickly succumbing to absolute bafflement. "Syd wasn't doing anything really," he says. "He was just sitting on the front of the stage, kicking his legs. It was very, very odd."

"My initial ambition was just to get them into some sort of shape," Gilmour later recalled. "It seems ridiculous now, but I thought the band was awfully bad at the time when I joined. The gigs I'd seen with Syd were incredibly undisciplined. The leader figure was falling apart, and so was the group."

It did not take long for Pink Floyd to bow to the inevitable. In David Gilmour's recollection, Barrett's ejection from the group was confirmed as they drove from London to an engagement in Southampton. "Someone said, 'Shall we pick up Syd?'" he later remembered, "and someone else said, 'Nah, let's not bother.' And that was the end."

So it was that Pink Floyd dispensed with the figure on whose talents their reputation had been built. "We carried on without a second thought," says Nick Mason. "It didn't occur to us that it wouldn't work. In retrospect, I find that very curious."

(opposite) David Gilmour joins the short-lived five-piece Floyd, January 1968. "The leader figure was falling apart, and so was the group," he later reflected. Left to right: Syd Barrett, David Gilmour, Rick Wright, Nick Mason, and Roger Waters (reclining). (Nick Mason's Archive)

2
HANGING ON IN QUIET DESPERATION:
ROGER WATERS AND PINK FLOYD MARK II

With Barrett gone, the creative leadership of Pink Floyd initially seemed to be up for grabs. The first recorded work they released in the wake of his exit was Rick Wright's almost unbearably whimsical "It Would Be So Nice," a single whose lightweight strain of pop-psychedelia—akin, perhaps, to the music of such faux-counterculturalists as the Hollies and Monkees—rendered it a non-event that failed to trouble the British charts; as Roger Waters later recalled, "No one ever heard it because it was such a lousy record." Waters's own compositional efforts, however, were hardly more promising. "Julia Dream," the single's B-side, crystallized much the same problem: though the band evidently wanted to maintain the Syd Barrett aesthetic, their attempts sounded hopelessly lightweight.

As 1968 progressed, though Rick Wright continued to add songs to the group's repertoire, it was quickly becoming clear where power now lay: with Roger Waters, the figure who, even when Barrett was around, had always had pretensions to being the band's chief. "From day one, he always seemed to be the leader of the band," says Aubrey Powell. "He had a commanding

Waters at Abbey Road, working on *A Saucerful of Secrets*. "From day one, he always seemed to be the leader of the band." (Music Pictures)

presence. He could be quite brusque, *rude.*"

"Roger was always the organizational person," says Peter Jenner. "If I wanted anything done, I had to fix Roger. He always had the good ideas: he always knew what he wanted to do. He was the bossy one: the one I had to persuade, always, because he could also be obstructive. He was the strongest personality in that sense."

If such a character sketch suggests a mind with pretensions to omnipotence, Jenner also saw weaknesses in Waters's initial contribution to the band: his apparently stunted musical talent, and his failure to satisfy the Underground's codes of cool. "Roger was the worst musician," he says. "He couldn't tune his guitar, he was tone deaf, and he also had some of the most awful sartorial things when they started becoming psychedelic. The worst thing were these red trousers that he put some dingly-dangly gold trim on, along the bottoms: the kind of thing you put on curtains. And he had a cigarette lighter in a sort of holster, dangling from his belt. He was terribly [uncool], Roger. *Terribly* naff. But he thought he was groovy."

Despite their friendship, the differences between Waters and Syd Barrett had tended to make them look like the occupants of completely different worlds. Barrett's '67-era personality was detached, non-materialistic, increasingly astral; Waters, by contrast, affected a hard-headed drive. One had become a living embodiment of the '60s counterculture; the other chose to guardedly keep his distance. Perhaps most tellingly of all, whereas Barrett's drug intake was disastrously prodigious—not simply in terms of his fondness for acid, but also when it came to marijuana and the British downer Mandrax—Waters was a drinker who rarely consumed anything illicit.

"I always remember being at the UFO club one night," recalls Aubrey Powell. "Syd was there, and Roger was there, backstage, and in walked Paul McCartney. It was a great revelatory moment: 'Fuck me—a Beatle's come to see the Pink Floyd.' *Really* something else. He was smoking a joint, and he passed it on. And Roger, who I'd never seen smoke before, took a huge hit of it. He knew when to play the game."

By his own admission, Waters took acid on no more than a couple of occasions: most memorably, on a trip to Greece in 1966, with a party of friends that included Rick Wright. "I didn't not do it again because I had a bad time particularly: it was more to do with how powerful it was," he says. "I've since heard my kids talk about taking acid and going out, and I was thinking, '*Going out?* You don't *go out!*' Acid came out of the bottle: it was very much a case of taking your 600 milligrams or whatever and making sure that you stayed *in*. It was a sufficiently powerful experience that was your only option. In Greece, I took it, and thought I was coming out the other end, and went to the window in the room where I was—and I stood on the spot for another three hours [laughs]. Just *frozen*."

Waters's onstage persona amounted to an approximation of poker-faced cool: recalling a Floyd concert at UFO in 1967, the Who's Pete Townshend once made reference to "Roger Waters and his impenetrable leer." In his early encounters with the press, he attempted to bolster the image with a hint of menace—"I lie and am rather aggressive," he told one interviewer. Underneath the hardened exterior, however, there was a good deal of fear.

"I was that guy in the black T-shirt and jeans, standing in the corner in dark glasses, smoking cigarettes and scowling at people," says Waters, "not wanting to have anything to do with anyone, 'cos I was so frightened. I think a lot it came down to a fear of being exposed; being found out. Mainly sexual exposure, I think; I suppose a lot of it was to do with sex.

52

Waters, the reluctant psychedelicist.
"I was that guy in the corner, scowling
at people, 'cos I was so frightened."
(Music Pictures)

Having grown up in the 1950s as an English teenager…well, there was a tremendous amount of repression hanging over all that stuff. I was far too ashamed to think about going into a barber shop and asking for a packet of condoms; I'd rather have died. It seems fucking ludicrous, but that's how it was. So you had this mixture of embarrassment, and the fear of pregnancy hanging over you, and it was hard to shrug a lot of that off."

Perhaps most importantly, whereas the story of Syd Barrett's childhood is full of the idyllic, familial warmth reflected in such Pink Floyd songs as "Matilda Mother," Waters's upbringing had been riven by the fault-line created by the death of his father. In January 1944, Eric Fletcher Waters had been killed at Anzio, Italy, during a battle for a beachhead that lasted four months and was later described as "the Allies' greatest blunder of World War II." He died aged thirty, leaving a family that had only just come into being: his wife, Mary, and two young children: Roger, five months, and an elder son named John. "As soon as I could talk, I was asking where my daddy was," Waters later reflected. "And my mother has often told me that when I was about two-and-a-half or three years old, it became really acute. In 1946, everyone got demobbed. Suddenly all these men appeared…they were picking their kids up from nursery school, and I became extremely agitated."

In the long term, the death of Waters's father seemed to foster an instinctive mistrust of authority, clearly evident during Waters's school years. "I don't necessarily know who I blamed for my father's death: a lot of my blame was focused on the Germans; the *enemy*," he says. "But I think if you look at my behavior at school, it may be that there was an element of not having a male authority figure in my home life, and therefore resisting the idea of anyone else taking on that role. That was probably a factor." By the time Waters became an architecture student at Regent Street Polytechnic, his irreverence had been combined with an aura of headstrong self-confidence: in the words of Nick Mason, "he sported an expression of scorn for the rest of us, which even the staff found off-putting."

The details of Waters's father's military service lent his story a particularly tragic aspect. In the early years of World War II, Eric Fletcher's Christianity led him into conscientious objection, meaning that he was exempted from the draft and given a job as an ambulance driver. As the war went on, however, he was drawn toward left-wing politics—and, eventually, the British Communist Party. Given the avowed opposition of communists to fascism, he performed a volte-face and joined the army as an officer; in that sense, his newfound political outlook cost him his life. "To have had the courage to not go—and then to change your mind and have the courage to go … is a sort of mysteriously heroic thing to have done," Waters later reflected.

In the years following the war, Mary Waters remained a communist, until the unforeseen events that caused thousands of Western European communists to renounce the party. "My mother lasted until 1956, when the Russians invaded Hungary," says Waters. "I don't remember that myself, but I became aware of it later on. That was a breaking point for a lot of people. But she was very hostile towards America. Not Americans themselves: she spent time in the USA when she was young and said that she had a tremendous amount of empathy with the people she met—but America's economic system and their role in the world.

"I can remember a lot of meetings of the British-Chinese Friendship Association; a lot of gatherings at the Quaker Meeting House in Cambridge. How much of it did I take on? Oh, I completely took it on lock, stock, and barrel. Unquestioningly. I think that's the nature of one's relationship with one's parents' politics. That's probably the one thing that youthful rebellion actually leaves in place. I was involved in the Young Socialists—I believed a lot of the same things."

In retrospect, Waters's personal history provided him with a rich seam of creative inspiration, and a singular, deeply English lyrical voice. In early 1968, however, those who had overseen Pink Floyd's progress were unimpressed by the idea of the group falling under his leadership. For Peter

Jenner and Andrew King, Syd Barrett's exit spelled the end of their hopes for the band; much to the Floyd's dismay, Jenner and King told them that their management role was at an end. Control of the band's affairs thus passed to the band's agent, Bryan Morrison. In time, the band's management would be taken over by Steve O'Rourke, a sometime Morrison employee regarded by Roger Waters as "an effective hustler … a man in a man's world."

"For us, it was, 'What the fuck are we going to do if Syd's not there?'" says Peter Jenner. "The answer was, as far as I recall, a look of pain: 'What do you mean? Aren't we worth anything?' 'Well, no—you're not. You're fucking no good. You can't tune your guitar, you can't sing.' The only hope was Rick—which is why, in the early post-Syd period, Rick did more of the writing. But he was more of an arranger. Nick couldn't write songs, and Roger, as far as I was concerned, was a non-musician. I certainly didn't think he could get away with singing: he couldn't pitch or anything. And I didn't know what to make of Dave, because he was just a dep, coming in to do Syd.

"We underestimated Roger's ability to understand what was going on, have a grip on it, and come up with a vision," he says. "And we failed to find out what Dave could do."

Part of the late-adolescent bohemian Cambridge crowd that had also included Roger Waters and Syd Barrett, David Gilmour had earned the quiet admiration of his peers by becoming a professional musician when his contemporaries were still taking their first tentative steps. With a five-man group named Jokers Wild—fond of such covers as Chuck Berry's "Beautiful Delilah" and the Four Seasons' "Big Girls Don't Cry"—he had established himself on Cambridge's limited gig circuit and even managed the dizzying transition to regular shows in London. "Dave was a good guitarist, he had quite a good voice, and he'd got his act together," says Aubrey Powell, another one of his Cambridge contemporaries. "His band was the most professional band in Cambridge, without question. I think the only other professional band was Bern Elliott and the Fenmen [laughs]. So Dave was revered, a little."

Aside from his musical prowess, Gilmour's social standing was boosted by two other factors: a precocity based on the fact that, given that his parents had relocated to the United States on account of his father's work as a geneticist, Gilmour lived in an apartment of his own—as well as his appeal to Cambridge's more switched-on women. "Dave always had a confidence: a quiet confidence," says Powell. "He's very good-looking, and he was *incredibly* good-looking in those days. You were very conscious that all the beautiful girls gravitated towards him."

By 1967, Jokers Wild had evolved—via a period spent trading under the self-consciously psychedelic name Flowers—into a trio called Bullitt, a short-lived enterprise that ended when Gilmour was called in to display his talents to an increasingly desperate Pink Floyd. He was keenly aware of their predicament: though once sufficiently close to Syd Barrett that the pair had busked their way around the south of France, he had paid his old compadre a social visit in May 1967 and found Barrett in such a frazzled state that their friendship did not even appear to be a distant memory. "They were recording and he told me to go the studio," he later remembered. "And I went down there and he didn't even recognize me."

According to Peter Jenner, at least some of Gilmour's appeal to the Floyd was based on the fact that he could do an eerily accurate imitation of his estranged friend. "I remember Dave being auditioned in Abbey Road," he says. "Somebody said, 'Come on Dave, give us your Hendrix.' And out came this extraordinary sound; quite breathtaking. That was the thing, though: Dave was a great mimic. He could play like Hendrix—and more importantly, he could do Syd, vocally and instrumentally."

The imperative to cover for Barrett, however, melted away with his exit from the band—and gradually, Pink Floyd found that Gilmour's presence was gently pushing them somewhere new. Whereas Barrett had made them brittle and chaotic, Gilmour infused their longer songs with a new sense of confidence and grace. As a result, they pulled back from the outer reaches of the avant-garde and became slightly more approachable, molding music that was simultaneously exploratory and open-ended, but firmly rooted in some kind of orthodoxy. "After Syd, Dave was the difference between light and dark," Nick Mason later recalled. "He was absolutely into form and shape, and he introduced that into the wilder numbers we created. We became far less difficult to enjoy."

As far as the group's internal chemistry was concerned, Gilmour had virtues that neatly complemented both Roger Waters and Rick Wright. Relative to the former, he was equipped with exactly the kind of musical nous that many claimed Waters lacked. With Wright, meanwhile, he formed a bond based on their shared, seemingly innate grasp of melody and structure. As in the Barrett line-up, Nick Mason's role was bound up less with creativity—he was, after all, some distance from being any kind of virtuoso—and had more to do with the personal qualities that infused the band with a much-needed human warmth. "Nick was Roger's mate, and he was always very civilized," says Peter Jenner. "A charmer. And he didn't make waves: he kept his head down."

"It's very hard to analyze what makes things work," says David Gilmour. "We had Rick, who wasn't a very driven person, but had a very good musical brain: he would sit and plonk away, and a lot of the time he would play very beautiful pieces. Roger had fantastic drive, and a very good brain for lyrics. He was a very driving, creative force. It did work very well."

If the new Pink Floyd was beginning to creatively cohere, in the wake of Syd Barrett's departure, it took them a long time to decisively escape his shadow. Their set lists still featured a handful of Barrett-era originals: "Interstellar Overdrive" was a dependable staple of their shows, and "Astronomy Domine" and "Pow R Toc H" would regularly join it. On occasion, meanwhile, the promotional grind found them pretending to be the group they no longer were: as in February 1968, when a Belgian television station insisted that a series of mimed performances include songs recorded the previous year. So it was that Gilmour bowed to the inevitable and dutifully lip-synched to such quintessential Barrett songs as "Scarecrow," "See Emily Play," and "Apples and Oranges."

Barrett's lingering ghost was also present on *A Saucerful of Secrets,* the album sporadically put to tape from late 1967 onwards, released in June 1968, and effectively launched by the Floyd's appearance at a vast free concert in London's Hyde Park. His own "Jugband Blues" was exhumed and used as the album's finale, thus lending it the air of a belated good-bye; chroniclers of the more arcane aspects of Pink Floyd's history have long discussed rumors that his guitar parts are meshed into Wright's "Remember a Day" and Waters's "Set the Controls for the Heart of the Sun." All that apart, one only need listen to Gilmour's nasal, knowingly English vocals on "Let There Be More Light," the Roger Waters song that acts as the album's overture—and is founded on a bass figure lifted from the middle section of "Interstellar Overdrive"—to understand that Pink Floyd still felt duty-bound to follow Barrett's example.

In his absence, however, changes were audibly underway. Most notably, though the album's two Rick Wright songs staked a gentle claim for the kind of melodic sensibility that had been one of Barrett's hallmarks, his efforts were largely swamped by the new music's vast dimensions. Waters's burgeoning leadership had one particularly clear upshot: either the new Pink Floyd had no wish to try to write pop songs, or were pretty much incapable of it. Instead, there was an evident wish to get to grips with the mastery of atmosphere, a quest most successfully realized on "Set the Controls," "Let There Be More Light," and the twelve-minute instrumental title track—so abstract and atonal that parts of it strayed close to being pretty much unlistenable, although David Gilmour has identified it as the seed of music that would arrive a little later on. "That was the first clue to our direction forwards," he later said. "If you take *A Saucerful of Secrets,* the track 'Atom Heart Mother,' then the track 'Echoes'—all lead quite logically towards *Dark Side of the Moon.*"

By way of setting out another one of the new Pink Floyd's hallmarks, responsibility for the album's artwork had been taken from EMI's in-house designers and handed to Waters and Gilmour's old Cambridge contacts Storm Thorgeson and Aubrey Powell, freshly established as sleeve designers under the achingly countercultural name Hipgnosis (mercifully, they had decided against trading as Consciousness Incorporated). Their design featured only a tiny image of the band; far more important, it seemed, were a slew of rather more exotic elements. "Being part of the early psychedelic era, we were interested in drugs, Marvel comics, zodiacs, montages, collages, and the whole Eastern essence that had drifted into the hippie movement," Powell later reflected.

One of *Saucerful's* most prophetic aspects rarely attracts comment. Roger Waters's "Corporal Clegg" may have been a rather directionless burlesque about an English war hero who "had a wooden leg," an impression only furthered by a deeply irritating passage played on kazoos—but it also served to make a point to which its author would return time and again: that underneath the stoic good cheer of English life there lurked a mess of dysfunction and sadness (an implication found particularly in its middle section, when Mrs. Clegg is coldly offered "another drop of gin"). Its lyric also dates the loss of its hero's limb to 1944—the same year that had seen the killing of Eric Fletcher Waters. In that sense, for all its pantomimic absurdity, it gave notice that Waters was prepared to root his songs in distinctly autobiographical sources.

That song's flawed attempt at storytelling also threw one of *Saucerful's* key shortcomings into sharp relief. On *The Piper at the Gates of Dawn,* Pink Floyd had minted a distinct aesthetic identity, founded not only on their improvisational aspects, but also on the singular elements that Syd Barrett brought to their music—not least, lyrics that somehow fused the hallucinatory mindset of psychedelia with the ghosts of his childhood. In

their place, there was very little at all; the new Pink Floyd had grasped matters of form and shape, but within most of their songs, there lurked an intellectual vacuum.

"Nick and Roger drew out *A Saucerful of Secrets* as an architectural diagram, in dynamic forms rather than any sort of musical form, with peaks and troughs," David Gilmour later remembered. "That's what it was about. It wasn't music for beauty's sake or emotion's sake."

"I don't think it's wrong if someone well-known uses his position to get over his beliefs, or influence people," David Gilmour mused in November 1969. "Why shouldn't he? We're just not very good at writing that kind of song. We never really set out specifically to protest about violence or anything. We don't want to come across with some incredible message. How would I define our music? There's not really much to explain. I don't know why it works out like it does. There's no special thing we deliberately work out. We're just trying to move ahead, to get things done."

Within his words, one senses the post–Syd Barrett Pink Floyd's central problem: a dogged attempt to maintain the group's momentum, compromised by the fact that their lack of any hard-and-fast ideas left them rather rudderless. Waters's burgeoning compositional talent was still in its infancy, leaving the band's lyrical ideas worryingly vague; compounding the problem, Gilmour and Rick Wright seemed less than interested in addressing the problem. "Rick used to do interviews and say that he didn't really care about lyrics," says Waters. "I used to read this stuff and think, 'Well, speak for yourself.' That did get quite frustrating. I think he liked to think of himself as a kind of musical purist. As did Dave." Nearly forty years on, Waters's frustration with his colleagues can still resurface. "They'd no fucking idea what the band was *for,*" he protests. In that sense, their first recording work of 1969 played to their limited strengths: their music for the Barbet Schroeder film *More,* knocked out in a mere eight days, managed a diverting mixture of muscular rock and ambient ethereality—but was as short on character as most low-budget film scores.

In fairness to the rest of the band, Waters hardly seemed to have a clear idea of exactly what he had to say to the world. The shortcomings of *A Saucerful of Secrets* set the pattern: for the moment, content took second place to a series of grand schemes that related to questions of shape and structure. In April 1969, for example, Pink Floyd played the first show that used the grandly named Azimuth Coordinator, a 360-degree sound set-up constructed to bathe their audience in music. Their interviews were quickly filled with enthusiastic pronouncements on the rather dry subject of what amounted to a souped-up PA system. "The idea," said Roger Waters, "is to put the sound all round all the audience with ourselves in the middle … like stereo, but forty times more effective."

A common response to Pink Floyd's evident interest in technology—coupled with the overtones of such songs as "Set the Controls for the Heart of the Sun"—was to characterize them as a band that specialized in the musical equivalent of science fiction, a stereotype they frequently seemed only too happy to fulfill. "We all read sci-fi and groove to *2001*," said Gilmour; Waters claimed that "there's nothing I'd like to do more than the music for Arthur C. Clarke's next screenplay." In July 1969, they appeared on a BBC TV special, screened to celebrate the imminent landing of Apollo 11 on the moon.

Occasionally, however, they seemed to be groping toward music that somehow reflected the trials of earthly existence. In April 1969, they premiered two suites entitled *The Man* and *The Journey,* made up of music that was already familiar to the band's public, and much that had yet to be released. The latter was a rather indistinct piece, which concluded in a three-part suite taking in "The Labyrinths of Auximenes," "Behold the Temple of Light," and "The End of the Beginning"; the former, featuring mind-boggling segments in which the group cut up pieces of wood and listened to a radio, found Waters attempting to represent the inhuman grind of everyday life.

The Azimuth Coordinator: "Like stereo, but 40 times more effective."
(Nick Mason's Archive)

The Man, he says, was at least partly based on graffiti that he saw each day on the London subway. "It was inspired," he enthuses. "It said, 'Get up, go to work, do your job, come home, go to bed, get up, go to work …' It was on this wall, and it seemed to go on forever, and as the train sped up, it would go by quicker and quicker until—bang!—you suddenly went into a tunnel. I just thought it was a brilliant work of art. Some of what we did with *The Man* was a little inspired by that; the wood part was meant to represent work. There was another element that involved switching on a transistor radio and putting it through the PA. Whatever was on would just blast out. The audience loved it. I'm not sure bands now would even *think* about doing something like that."

In its wake came the first proper post-Barrett album: *Ummagumma,* released in October 1969. Here, the problems that had so bedeviled *A Saucerful of Secrets* had hardly been cured. Thanks partly to the ill-advised idea of dividing its composition among all four members, large chunks of it came dangerously close to sounding like commercial suicide: the abstract, faux-classical suite Rick Wright titled "Sysyphus"; Nick Mason's yawn-inducing percussive piece "The Grand Vizier's Garden Party"; a baffling attempt at comedy by Roger Waters called "Several Species of Small Furry Animals Gathered Together in a Cave and Grooving with a Pict" (if Waters didn't smoke much marijuana, it certainly sounded like it). As if to acknowledge that the idea gave their public short weight, half the package was given over to a live album, on which the specter of Syd Barrett made a somewhat inevitable appearance: by way of reminding the band's audience that this was the same group that had made such inspired music a couple of years before, it began with a rendition of "Astronomy Domine," testament to David Gilmour's admirable talent for mimicry.

In fairness, there was a lot of such poorly realized, loose-ended stuff around in 1969. It was also the year that John Lennon and Yoko Ono released the unlistenable *Life with the Lions* and *Wedding Album,* and Bob Dylan began work on the wilfully awful *Self-Portrait*—albums that sought, in their own ill-advised way, to test both their audience's expectations and the limits of musical orthodoxy. Lennon and Dylan, however, had sufficiently towering artistic reputations to risk a momentary detour into creative lunacy; whether a group in the position of the post-Barrett Floyd should have tried it is another matter. That said, the fragrant aroma of psychedelia still hung around large swaths of their audience, meaning that even their most quixotic music tended to be received with a generosity of spirit that different times would probably have denied them. In response to *Ummagumma,* for example, the British DJ and hippie monarch John Peel worked himself into raptures over its "incredibly melancholy sounds, which cross one another sounding like crowds of dying galaxies lost in sheer corridors of time and space."

The Floyd was also blessed to be working in a musical culture in which the process of a band finding its artistic feet could be hastened by the sheer velocity of its schedule. By early 1970, *Ummagumma* was but a memory: the music that would find its way onto *Atom Heart Mother* was in progress, and they had spent time in Rome working on the soundtrack to Michelangelo Antonioni's movie *Zabriskie Point,* an attempt to crystallize his belief that in the late 1960s, the era of the Vietnam War, the United States was in the midst of an unprecedented cultural conflict. Despite their best efforts, the four Englishmen he chose for the task couldn't seem to deliver what he wanted: "We did some great stuff," Roger Waters later remembered, "but he'd listen and go, 'Eet's very beautiful but eet's too sad,' or 'Eet's too strong.' It was always wrong, consistently. You'd change whatever was wrong and he was still unhappy."

Listening to much of what was recorded, it's hard to avoid the conclusion that Antonioni had precious little musical nous at all. Among the ideas he rejected was a solo piano piece Rick Wright composed for a scene based around a campus riot: a beautifully serene six minutes, played with an accomplished sense of understatement, that acted as a compelling counterpoint to the images it accompanied. The so-called Violent Sequence was an early tryout of the music that later formed the basis of "Us and Them" from *The Dark Side of the Moon;* even in its embryonic form, it oozed much of the same affecting magic that would be so spectacularly realized

(Nick Mason's Archive)

two years later. The group certainly had confidence in it: as of January 1970, it regularly found its way into their shows.

At around the same time as the band was clashing with Antonioni, Roger Waters served notice of their next move. "We want to write a complete work for an orchestra and ourselves," he told the *NME,* "so that the group is another part of the orchestra." The Floyd's mechanistic obsession with sound systems quickly reared its rather ugly head: "Then," Waters went on, "the orchestra would be split up and positioned around the hall—along with the speakers— so the audience would be sitting in the middle of the music."

The result of such ambitions was "Atom Heart Mother," the twenty-three-minute piece that would form the lion's share of Pink Floyd's next album. First put to tape in the spring of 1970, it soon became a collaboration with Ron Geesin, an experimental composer and arranger—and alumnus of the '60s Underground. Geesin and Waters had bonded when they worked on the soundtrack for *The Body,* an experimental documentary movie on human biology (in addition to their musical activities, the pair were occasional golf partners). As the group prepared for a U.S. tour in April 1970, Geesin was handed a backing track provisionally entitled "Epic" and asked to augment it with an orchestra. As it turned out, he contributed much more, bolstering the piece's melodic aspect, and—on their return—tutoring the group in the use of sound effects and the creative aspects of tape editing. It was not the easiest of jobs: stress, combined with a sweltering British summer, led Geesin to carry out at least some of his work dressed only in his underpants.

The result, randomly named in honor of a newspaper headline, still sounds superficially impressive—lush, ambitious, compellingly unpredictable—but is rather hampered by its lack of any real sense of substance. The absence of any lyrics may be its key problem, but its various musical elements—very English brass, an overlong choral passage, an outbreak of avant-garde experimentation that sounds remarkably like the Beatles' "Revolution 9"—fail to mesh together, sounding less like the product of inspired thinking than a rather lazy exercise in cleverness for its own sake. That said, the piece does show hints of real promise, as evidenced by David Gilmour's delightful slide guitar playing (so redolent of *Dark Side* as to almost sound like a trailer), and a stripped-down passage—entitled "Funky Dung"—in which he and Rick Wright achieve a kind of easy, fluid virtuosity. The group, however, remains doubtful of "Atom Heart Mother"'s merits. "It was a real bit of cobbled-together old rubbish," admits Gilmour. "I really shouldn't say that—but there wasn't much clear thinking in our minds."

"Atom Heart Mother" formed the centerpiece of the album of the same name, packaged in a wonderful Hipgnosis sleeve, somehow both banal and surreal, that featured a color photograph of a solitary English cow. If, for all its skewed charm, it found the Floyd still bedeviled by the lack of purpose that had so plagued them since Syd Barrett's departure, there was at least one hint of a way out of the mire. No sooner had the title track drawn to a close than its slightly overwrought aftertaste was banished by a Roger Waters song simply entitled "If," delivered against the most pared-down of backing tracks in the composer's own fragile, plaintive half-voice.

"'If' is about not presenting the caring side of oneself, even to friends and loved ones," says Waters. "There are lines like, 'If I were a swan, I'd be gone/If I were a train I'd be late/If I were good man I'd talk to you more often than I do.' And there's also lines in there like 'If I were alone I'd cry/If I were with you I'd be home and dry/If I go insane, please don't put your wires in my brain.' I can hear some of what I did on *Dark Side of the Moon* in that."

If his retrospective understanding of "Atom Heart Mother" suggests that the band was steadily making progress toward its masterpiece, Waters's pronouncements from the time often exude a real pessimism—as if life in the Floyd was an increasingly unrewarding grind, and he was starting to question the band's worth. As he entered his late twenties, he occasionally seemed to believe that, for all his grand artistic designs, he was dangerously close to going through the motions, as he later put it—simply "in the pipeline, filling in time."

At the tail end of 1970, a journalist from *Melody Maker* visited Waters at the home in North London that he shared with his wife, Judy—a schoolteacher, amateur sculptor, and (according to at least one Floyd associate) "extreme leftie" whom he had married in 1969—and six Burmese cats. "Being married," he explained, "makes things much simpler. It makes it easier to cope what's important and what isn't. It sorts out your priorities."

From the outside, the house seemed no different from the other Victorian buildings with which it shared the street. Inside, however, there lay clear evidence of a mind in tune with rather more voguish currents. "All is modernity," said the writer, "that fashionable kind with bare polished wood floors and Scandinavian furniture that immediately hits the eyes because of its clean, spare lines. Mr. Waters used to study architecture, and he has got taste, you see." In the garden, there was a "garden-cum-tool-shed," given over to both Waters's home demo studio, and a jumble of objects and equipment put to artistic use by his wife.

Pink Floyd was about to set off on a European tour, taking in Holland, West Germany, Switzerland, Austria, and France. The planned shows included such increasingly tired staples as "Astronomy Domine," "Set the Controls for the Heart of the Sun," and "A Saucerful of Secrets," along with a stripped-down version of "Atom Heart Mother" and Gilmour's recent composition "Fat Old Sun." Unfortunately, the inclusion of relatively new songs—not to mention the recent success of *Atom Heart Mother,* which had made it to the top of the British albums chart—hardly seemed to ease Waters's sense of impending tedium. "I'm bored with most of the stuff we've done," he said. "I'm bored with most of the stuff we play… there isn't much new stuff, is there?"

By the interview's midpoint, he was sounding positively jaded. "It's a job: a fucking well-paid job, with all the ego-boosting stuff and everything, and I think it becomes very mechanical," he spat. "I'm going off on a 10-date tour tomorrow, right? Frankfurt, Vienna, Montreux—but why am I going? To spread the gospel, to make people happy by playing them wonderful music?

"No, it's not true," he concluded. "I'm going to make some bread. I'm going because I'm caught up in the whole pop business machinery."

Prior to his move to North London, Waters had lived in Pennard Mansions, an enclosed apartment block that lies at the eastern end of Goldhawk Road, a shabby, cosmopolitan strip that links the inner-city London neighborhood of Shepherd's Bush with the altogether more upmarket enclave of Chiswick. The area—scratched into rock lore thanks to its association with the Who—has long had a bustling, hectic ambience focused chiefly on a huge local street market. For the young Waters, who lived in a tiny apartment there for the early phase of Pink Floyd's post–Syd Barrett existence, the area crystallized his feelings about the allure and quiet terror of life in the city, and what it might say about the human condition.

"I lived there with the childhood sweetheart who was later to become my wife," says Waters. "And in the absence of Syd, when I was beginning to start writing … I have a very strong mental picture of a window in the apartment, with sunlight coming through it, and feeling a strong sense of being in the city. I was really a country boy; I hadn't been in London all that long. And I had a kind of underlying concern about how much human beings do or don't foster their capacity for empathy. Living in

The live Floyd, pre–*Dark Side*. "I'm bored with most of the stuff we play," Roger Waters complained. Clockwise from top left: Roger Waters (Nick Mason's Archive/Studio Conreur), David Gilmour (Nick Mason's Archive/John Austin), Rick Wright (Rex Features), Nick Mason (Nick Mason's Archive).

London seemed to throw that into sharper relief."

Surveying the human traffic of Goldhawk Road from the confines of his room, Waters came up with a poetic, if rather whimsical, lyric that dealt with the possibility, in the midst of London's impersonal tumult, of two people at least making momentary contact: "Strangers passing in the street, by chance two separate glances meet/And I am you, and what I see is me." On the face of it, the lines skirt dangerously close to hippie platitude, yet they served to establish an aspect of Pink Floyd's universe that would stay there for the best part of the next decade. "They expressed a preoccupation that I'd had, and I was going to continue to have," says Waters, "with the potential that human beings have for recognizing each other's humanity and responding to it, with empathy rather than antipathy. That fundamental notion is what that lyric deals with."

If the words served to belatedly establish their author's most passionate concerns, the music to which they were eventually set pulled off an even greater set of feats: pulling Pink Floyd out of the underachievement that had blighted much of its work since the departure of Syd Barrett, allowing it to finally firm up its sense of identity, avenging an increasing sense of jadedness, and thereby propelling it toward the wonders of *The Dark Side of the Moon*. Such was the pivotal importance of the sixteen-minute piece they eventually titled "Echoes" and used as the bedrock of 1971's *Meddle*.

If all that suggests some gleaming triumph, however, this phase of Pink Floyd's progress was initially marked by an all too familiar difficulty: a creeping sense of confusion and paralysis, as the band fretted about what exactly they should do next. "I can remember an irritation that we didn't seem able to get a grip on anything," says Nick Mason. "There was a sense that we couldn't seem to get things started. Once it was rolling, then it happened. But getting started was always the problem."

In January 1971, John Leckie was a twenty-one-year-old junior engineer on the payroll of Abbey Road studios, who had cut his teeth as a tape operator on such albums as George Harrison's *All Things Must Pass* and Ringo Starr's *Sentimental Journey,* as well as working as an engineer on *John Lennon/Plastic Ono Band.* He was an exemplar of a new culture that was taking root at Abbey Road, as its staff left behind the fusty, uptight practices that had taken root well before the advent of rock 'n' roll, and became more attuned to the lifestyles of the musicians with whom they worked. "That was how I got the job, really," he says. "They liked the fact that I had long hair. If you came in on a Saturday and saw an older engineer, instead of having a suit and tie, he'd be wearing a sports jacket and an open-neck shirt. You'd be thinking, 'Wow! I've never seen you without a tie!' A lot of the people there were very … *straight.*"

As part of Abbey Road's new school, Leckie eventually found himself employed as a tape-op on the sessions for *Meddle,* not least because of Pink Floyd's fondness for working into the small hours. "Anything after 5:30 P.M. was counted as overtime," he says. "And with a lot of sessions, the older guys would turn them down, 'cos they didn't want to stay up all night. Of course, I did."

As it turned out, the Floyd—initially, at least—did not lay on quite the all-night creative spectacular that Leckie could have been forgiven for expecting. "Pink Floyd sessions had a reputation for being boring," he later reflected. "You might start at two in the afternoon and not finish till four in the morning, during which time nothing would get done. There was no record company contact whatsoever, except when their label manager would show up now and again with a couple of bottles of wine and a couple of joints. That was it. They had a little cocktail bar in the studio, with a fridge, and a fair bit of tequila and Southern Comfort was drunk, but there wasn't a lot of chemical abuse going on. The atmosphere wasn't unfriendly, but there would be long silences; periods of boredom."

"Some days," says Leckie, "they would spend a lot of time just working on one sound, or a single guitar riff. And very often, they wouldn't say much to each other. Then they'd suddenly get very excited about something, and you wouldn't quite know why—or they'd get something taped, and they wouldn't like it, and you'd be thinking, 'Well, what was wrong with that?' There was a lot of that going on … and a general sense of frustration."

In Leckie's recollection, the sessions for *Meddle* began with the band "searching for things." Cloistered in Abbey Road in January 1971, they decided to begin filling tape with anything that sounded promising, from single sounds—like a piano note, fed through a revolving Leslie speaker—to random snatches of music. Eventually, this rather loose-ended project was given a name—perhaps indicating a worrying dearth of inspiration, the Floyd called their work-in-progress "Nothing: Parts 1 to 24." In March, David Gilmour took the concept a little further: the next Floyd album, he told a British journalist, had the working title "Return of the Son of Nothing."

Compounding the sense that they were distractedly treading water, the group used further sessions at Air Studios—a central London facility owned by the sometime Beatles producer George Martin, which had sixteen-track machines as against Abbey Road's eight-track equipment—to attempt the kind of mind-boggling idea that might have been more at home on *Ummagumma:* music made using a variety of household objects. "There were about four days spent on that," says Leckie. "They were making chords up from the tapping of beer bottles. And tearing paper, and letting off aerosol cans. Those things were aimed at sounding like hi-hats. It didn't seem to be going anywhere." In addition, sessions were regularly interrupted when the Floyd packed up their equipment and headed out of London. "They were always off gigging, having to pack the gear up and go off and play a gig and come back again," says Leckie. "Very much a band on the road."

Eventually, however, they alighted on a way forward. Listening back to the "Nothing" fragments, resolving to segue some of them together into one continuous piece, and seizing on the lyrics that Waters had written in

Pennard Mansions, they came up with a composition of unprecedented power and imagination. Just about all of its segments pulsed with the right stuff: its initial mellifluous, drifting section, in which Waters's two-strangers scenario (along with Barrett-esque images of "coral caves" and "rolling waves") was accorded a suitably dreamlike backdrop; a hard-edged, R'n'B–tinged interlude, frosted with wonderfully scabrous solos from Gilmour, that developed the side of the band's music that had surfaced on "Funky Dung" from *Atom Heart Mother;* and a passage immediately before final reprise of the first section, in which the Floyd achieved a quite unprecedented synthesis of dexterity and sheer musical power. "I was amazed when they came in about a month later, and they'd tagged it all together," says Leckie. "It sounded incredible."

"Echoes"—initially entitled "Return of the Son of Nothing"—was given its first live performance on April 22, 1971, at a show in the East English city of Norwich. Its grand premiere, meanwhile, came just under a month later, when Pink Floyd headlined an outdoor "Garden Party"— supported by the Faces, Quiver, and Mountain—at the Crystal Palace Bowl in South London. The weekly British music press was pretty much unanimous in its praise for the group's latest creation; the only dissenting voice came from a rather mealymouthed reporter from the *Croydon Advertiser,* who claimed that it "didn't come across on first hearing as being particularly distinguished."

Back in the studio, John Leckie recalls the group resuming work with a drive and vision that in January had been all but absent. "The power clearly lay with Roger," he says. "He sat behind the desk the whole time. Dave was the second in command; the more creative, musical one. But Roger effectively took the role of producer. Rick Wright didn't say much. And Nick Mason was very much the comedian. He lightened things up."

"Echoes" was gradually taken to completion, benefiting not only from its concerted rehearsal and live performances but from the kind of technological ingenuity that the Floyd had been honing since the Syd Barrett

London, fall 1971. "The power clearly lay with Roger. Dave was the second in command. Rick Wright didn't say much. And Nick Mason lightened things up." (Nick Mason's Archive)

period. "We had two stereo tape machines on either side of the room," says Leckie. "We put the tape on the first machine, and then ran it maybe five feet across the room on to a second machine, with both of them recording. The signal started on the first machine, and much as eight or nine seconds later, it would come out of the next one—and then feed back. You could sit there for hours, with everything you played being repeated; and after a while, incredible things would start to happen. The abstract bit at the end of "Echoes"—the part that sounds kind of *choral*—was done like that."

In retrospect, the group have little doubt of the importance of "Echoes" to their history. "Thematically, lyrically and musically, and in terms of its construction," says Roger Waters, "it was a foretaste of what was to come."

"'Echoes' was a successful blueprint," agrees David Gilmour. "For me, there's a big jump between *Atom Heart Mother* and *Meddle,* and 'Echoes' in particular. Then again, it's another quite large leap from that to *Dark Side of the Moon*—but you can see the direction we were moving in."

The new piece took up an entire side of *Meddle,* leaving room for a mixed collection of supporting features; its two other highpoints were "One of These Days," founded on the brilliantly potent sound of a Waters bass figure fed through ad echo unit, and the languid "Fearless," which tapped into the same sun-kissed ambience that Gilmour had captured on "Fat Old Sun." Released in November 1971, it ascended to Number 3 in the British albums chart, though in the United States its fate spoke volumes about the commercial distance that the Floyd had still to travel: whereas *Atom Heart Mother* had climbed to a promising high point of 55, this new album could only make it to number 70. Such, it seemed, were the downsides of trading in what the *Washington Post* termed "the closest thing that rock music has to show in the way of the avant-garde."

Just prior to the album's appearance, the Floyd had staged a performance that only served to underwrite their high-art credentials. At the suggestion of a French film director named Adrian Maben, they made the journey—along with truckloads of equipment—to the ruined Roman city of Pompeii, in Southern Italy. There, they performed in the jaw-droppingly atmospheric surroundings of Pompeii's amphitheater. They were watched only by Maben's filming team and their own road crew. "I felt that we'd had enough of concert films," the director later explained. "So the main idea of the film was to do a sort of anti-Woodstock film, where there would be nobody present, and the music, and the silence, and the empty ampitheater would say as much—if not more—as a crowd of a million."

Though the movie, bolstered by additional sequences filmed in Paris, didn't quite fulfill such ambitious designs, it proved one thing beyond doubt: without any supporting cast, the Floyd—hardly the most animated rock band—could carry the film by the simple power of their performance. At *Live at Pompeii*'s peak moments—"One of These Days," "Careful with That Axe Eugene," a deeply impressive rendition of "Echoes"—they capably rose to such demands: proof, it seemed, of how far they had come since the departure of Syd Barrett.

The decisive leap from his shadow, however, lay just around the corner.

The set of *Live at Pompeii*, October 1971. "The main idea of the film was to do a sort of anti-Woodstock." (Nick Mason's Archive)

3

AND IF THE BAND YOU'RE IN STARTS PLAYING DIFFERENT TUNES:
THE DARK SIDE OF THE MOON IS BORN

The modern music industry has long since established a creative cycle for successful rock bands: albums are expected to arrive every two or three years, to be followed by concerted touring and promotional chores and—where necessary—the recovery periods known as "downtime." In 1971, however, the pace of musicians' lives was altogether more frenetic. Though the hyperactive frenzies of the early to mid-1960s—when the Beatles and Stones had dutifully knocked out two albums every twelve months—were long gone, rock bands were still expected to come up with a new collection of songs every year. Moreover, the imperative to play live rarely let up. Bob Dylan's admirers may have proclaimed his invention of the Never Ending Tour in the late 1980s; two decades before, a seemingly eternal concert schedule was simply part and parcel of the rock life.

In December 1971, Pink Floyd was a perfect case in point. Less than a month after the release of *Meddle*, the band assembled at Broadhurst Gardens in North West London, to spend time at one of their staple rehearsal studios. Faced with a seventeen-date British tour in the new year, to be followed by trips to Japan and the United States, they were desperate to add new material to their live repertoire. Even their most recent shows have found them falling back on such hoary staples as "Set the Controls for the Heart of the Sun," "Careful with That Axe Eugene," and "A Saucerful of Secrets." By now, even the eternally sanguine Nick Mason was succumbing to a sense of tedious inertia: he was, he told a British journalist, "dying of boredom."

There was also the looming prospect of recording a new album, though for now, the renewal of their live set was the priority. "In those days," says David Gilmour, "tours got booked in. And back then, they weren't promotional vehicles; they were entities in their own right. I don't know if we actually needed new songs, but it's always nice to have new stuff to do. The genesis of these things was that, every once in a while, we would convene in a good rehearsal space, and start knocking ideas about."

Though the Floyd had long since acquired a reputation as a group whose creativity was recurrently fired by the technology available in the studio, the experience of fine-honing "Echoes" proved that their music was often best served by the straight-ahead grind of playing live in a practice room. And so it proved, though their initial work at Broadhurst Gardens could occasionally fall into directionless torpor. "I'm not sure how much *writing* happened there," said Roger Waters. "You know, 'Let's play E minor and A for an hour or so.' 'Oh, all right—that'll fill up five minutes.'"

As was often their way, they began by rummaging through some of the odds and ends they had accumulated over the previous eighteen months— "plundering the rubbish library," as David Gilmour put it. In some cases, this was a matter of simply dusting down fragments of music that had lain idle—as with "The Violent Sequence," the Rick Wright piano music that Michelangelo Antonioni had rejected for *Zabriskie Point*. Here, Wright's impossibly serene composition was radically slowed down, and infused— chiefly in its central sections—with a new power: "It's very flowing and sweet if you look at the verse," he later reflected, "and then there's the contrast—this big, harder chorus." Similarly, the band also returned to a Wright-authored chord sequence—played on a churchy-sounding organ—that was newly tried out as an instrumental interlude variously known as "Religious Theme" and "Mortality Sequence."

In other cases, recent material was used as a jumping-off point rather than a musical source. The opening line of a new song entitled "Breathe" came from a track of the same name—a folky and not a little sardonic look at the problem of air pollution—that Waters and Ron Geesin had used for the soundtrack of *The Body;* its new setting was the two-chord jam to which Waters alludes above, based on chords that may or may not have been pilfered from Neil Young's "Down by the River," released in July 1969 (played back to back, the resemblance between the two is little short of hilarious). Its chorus, meanwhile, was founded on a descending chord sequence—the work of Rick Wright—that took it somewhere else entirely, partly thanks to his inspired use of a suspended piano chord he adopted from Miles Davis's *Kind of Blue.*

Inevitably, as the rehearsals went on, completely original compositions were added to the band's works-in-progress. "Time" began life as a washed-out Roger Waters home demo, played on an out-of-tune acoustic guitar—but when put to the band, was revived by an arrangement split between dolorous, downcast verses and a dreamlike middle section—and Nick Mason's inspired use of a set of rototoms: compact drums, tuned to specific notes that were put to brilliant use on the song's intro. Waters's off-the-cuff improvisation of a cyclical seven-note bass riff led to another home demo of "Money," initially written as a reedy kind of acoustic blues, only to eventually be transformed—thanks chiefly to the input of David Gilmour—into an uncharacteristically meaty piece of modernized R'n'B.

"Making *The Dark Side of the Moon,* we were all trying to do as much as we possibly could," says Roger Waters. "It was a very communal thing. What's that old Marxist maxim? 'From each according to his ability, to each according to his need.' That's sort of the way the band worked at that point."

If the new songs hinted at an artistic breakthrough, the decisive watershed came when Waters, tapping back into the fondness for grand designs that had defined "Atom Heart Mother" and "Echoes," came up with a striking suggestion: why not wrap the lyrics in one all-embracing theme? The scheme had two interlinked effects: music they had already worked on suddenly cohered, and Waters was inspired to add even more new material.

"I suspect that the big idea came before the writing of quite a number of the lyrics," he says. "I can remember explaining it to the rest of the band. Nick Mason had a house on St. Augustine's Road in Camden Town—I remember sitting in his kitchen and explaining this idea; that the whole record might be about the pressures and preoccupations that divert us from our potential for positive action, if you like." With the benefit of hindsight, Waters later summed up his theme as "an expression of political, philosophical, humanitarian empathy that was desperate to get out."

Subsequent explanations of Waters's concept have often been equally vague, a problem hardly helped by his colleagues' varied ideas of what he was driving at. "It was madness, I suppose—to put it briefly," says David Gilmour. "The pressures of modern living, and all the elements that one goes through that conspire to send some people insane." In Nick Mason's understanding, "the concept was originally about the pressures of modern life—travel, money, and so on—but then Roger turned it into a meditation on insanity." Rick Wright, meanwhile, saw the core of Waters's lyrics as a treatise "about the business," suffused with references to the life of a rock band.

When explaining what he was driving at, Waters himself has usually been voluble, though not exactly clear. "If there's any central message," he said in 2003, "it's this: this [i.e. life] is not a rehearsal. As far as we know, you only get one shot, and you've got to make choices based on whatever moral, philosophical, or political position you may adopt.... You make choices during your life, and those choices are influenced by political considerations and by money and by the dark side of all our natures. You get the chance to make the world a lighter or darker place in some small way. We all get the opportunity to transcend our tendencies to be self-involved and mean and greedy. We all make a small mark on the painting of life." What drew the songs of early 1972 together, he said, was "an exhortation to join in the flow of natural history … to embrace the positive and reject the negative."

The explanation amounts to a slightly verbose knot of mixed metaphor and fuzzy platitude—and yet it's not hard to survey Waters's various pronouncements about his grand theme and divine a central core. The Floyd's new song cycle seemed to be based on the old '60s Underground idea that society's ills were reflected in individual lives that had become—to use Richard Neville's phrase—"pinched and grey and silly and caught up with trivia." In elevating such man-made constructs as time and money to the point that they ended up controlling us, we had lost our grip on both what it was to be human—empathetic, compassionate, social—and arrived at such a contorted way of thinking that madness was close to being a logical consequence. To avoid such a fate, there was one possible way out: in Waters's words, to tap back into "some kind of gestalt being—the rebel or the child within us all—who embodies what's precious about us in our innocence when we're conceived, and what becomes subverted through living." In that sense, the piece's opening words were a kind of compact manifesto: "Breathe, breathe in the air/Don't be afraid to care."

Some of this had begun to bubble through his interviews over the previous two years. "I'm frightened of other people," he said in August 1970. "I don't think I know *anybody* who isn't frightened of other people. People know that if you lower your defenses, someone jumps on you. I find myself jumping on people all the time and regretting it afterwards … I haven't even begun to find out how to relate myself to the rest of the world, and people, and what to do about them." Three months later, he was asked about the root of the West's obsession with success and material gain. "The interesting thing is if we're born with it or not," he said. "If we're not, that means that it's foisted on us by the system." He wondered whether there was any prospect of a more enlightened way of living, before bleakly concluding that it was "impossible in our society, because we're pumped full of personal acquisitions."

Though Waters's thematic conceit was more than a little loose-ended, one aspect of Pink Floyd's new material was beyond doubt: within his concept and the songs it spawned, there lurked all kinds of autobiographical entrails. The underlying idea that the Industrial Age had estranged us from our innate attributes, for example, amounted to a reductive take on the Marxist concept of alienation[1]—an article of faith within the communism that had been embraced by his mother and father, and had so colored his upbringing. More specifically, the wry sideswipe at the tyranny of hard cash in "Money" could surely be traceable to the slightly ascetic beliefs that he had inherited from his parents.

Aside from all that, Mary Waters also inspired the lyric of "Time"— thanks to her own kind of alienated thinking. "I was twenty-nine in 1972," says Waters, "and it was a very powerful moment in my life. Very suddenly, it struck me: 'Fucking hell—this is *it*.' I had not understood that, because of the family that I came from. My upbringing was all about, 'You're going to want to get a decent job, because you won't want to be bored, and you're going to want to have a family, so you need to prepare—you need to get a decent education, and do this and do that.' This is my mother talking. Everything was always in order to prepare for real life, which was at some point going to start down the road. It came as a great shock to discover that I wasn't preparing for anything—I was right in the middle of it, and always had been."

Eric Fletcher Waters, meanwhile, made an appearance in "Us and Them," the gorgeous song Waters and Wright alchemized from "The Violent Sequence." According to Waters, its second and third verses respec-

[1] The requisite entry in *The Penguin Dictionary of Politics* (1985) contains the following explanation: "For Marx, alienation is a condition … where the human nature of man is made other than—alien to—what man is really capable of being.… Man could be alienated from himself, from other men, from his working life and from the product of his labour … all these are interconnected, and for Marx they all stem from the capitalist productive system."

tively dealt with "civil liberties, racism, and color prejudice" and "passing a tramp in the street and not helping." Most crucial, however, were opening stanzas that dealt with "going to war—how in the front line we don't get much chance to communicate with one another, because someone else has decided that we shouldn't." "Forward he cried from the rear/And the front rank died," went its lyric, "and the General sat/As the lines on the map moved from side to side." Here, it seems, Waters aimed at transporting the listener back to Anzio in January 1944.

As Rick Wright had divined, at least some of Waters's lyrics were rooted in a slightly more ephemeral place: the existence of a working rock group, replete with its attendant temptations and anxieties. These elements didn't quite fit with Waters's more philosophical concerns, but they sparked some of the new music's most impressive moments. The reprise of "Breathe," for example, was filled with the weariness of musicians plodding back from yet another tour: "Home, home again/I like to be here when I can." "Money," meanwhile, satirized the pretensions of the rock super-rich: "I'm in the high-fidelity first class travelling set/And I think I need a Lear jet." In its own way, the lyric provided an ironic take on something Waters had said around the time of the recording of *Meddle:* "I think there's a great danger in getting into that sports car bit. It's all very, very, very tricky and hard, and we have great arguments in the band about it, because I proclaim vaguely socialist principles, and I sit there spouting a lot of crap about how having a lot of bread worries me—and we are earning a lot of bread now. I couldn't be happy in an E-Type Jaguar, because it just seems all wrong, somehow. I mean, who needs 4.2 litres and a big shiny bonnet?"

More chillingly, Rick Wright's so-called Mortality Sequence, along with a frantic instrumental interlude entitled "The Travel Section"—initially based on a mesmeric rhythm guitar part played by Gilmour—were point-edly about the underlying fear of death that came with the Floyd's world-traversing travel schedules. "We spent a lot of our time on airplanes," says Roger Waters. "There weren't many professions where at a very young age, you'd spend that much time in the air. There's something about flight that appeals to us all, but is also quite frightening. 'The Travel Section' piece was about the terror of travel, and worrying that you're about to die—which at the end of it, you do. It was supposed to represent some sort of crash."

If Waters's lyrics found his questioning, dissenting sensibility applied to some of life's most inescapable aspects, his surrounding social and political environment only served to encourage him. The Vietnam War, the conflict that had so captured the imagination and incurred the wrath of the '60s counterculture, was not only still ongoing, but also wreaking its toxic political effects as never before: June 1971 had seen the publication of the Pentagon Papers, the "secret history" of America's role in Vietnam that exposed government deceit and skullduggery, turned yet more Americans against the conflict, and fed a sense of panic and paranoia in the Nixon White House—thus leading, in the wake of the 1972 presidential election, to the meltdown of Watergate.

In Waters's home country, meanwhile, the sense of national self-confidence that had powered thousands of Britons through the 1960s was starting to fade, as the altogether harsher realities of a new era—which would, in retrospect, stoke the fires of the British side of punk rock—began to take root. Waters was a daily reader of *The Guardian,* the U.K.'s upmarket liberal-left newspaper—and scanning its pages from the late summer of 1971 onwards, one gets a powerful sense of the context in which he was writing. That August, it was announced that British unemployment had reached 904,000—the highest level since the dread days of the 1930s. The terrorism practiced by Irish Republicans was also regularly impacting on the headlines: October saw an explosion at London's iconic Post Office Tower; in January 1972, the British army killed thirteen demonstrators on the day that came to be known as Bloody Sunday, and less than a month later, the paramilitary Irish Republican Army retaliated by killing six British servicemen in the southern English town of Aldershot.

Against that backdrop, the ideals that had defined the '60s counterculture were also under renewed attack. September 1971 saw the launching rally of a British organization called the Festival of Light, led by an already notorious campaigner called Mary Whitehouse, who had dedicated herself to rolling back the permissive attitudes of the previous decade, by way of an attack on "moral pollution" and the assertion of "Christian values." Waters was quietly appalled: "I was incensed by Mary Whitehouse," he said, "as I am by all book-burners and bible-bashers; people who foster that sexual guilt and shame, who try and deny people any opportunity to fulfill their sexual destiny."[2]

The same month, *The Guardian* ran a story about a recent government report that looked into work-related stress, a phenomenon just starting to grip the imagination of the popular media, and thereby begin its three-decade passage to the very center of the modern consciousness. If Waters was about to pour out his thoughts on "the pressures of modern living," here was proof of his concerns' topicality. "The numbers affected by psychosis, psycho-neurosis, as well as the less worrying complaints of debility, nervousness, and headaches have been soaring," said *The Guardian.* "According to the report, the best way to avoid trouble is to ensure the worker should be satisfied with his work, and should be stretched to his limits, but not beyond them."

Pink Floyd, of course, had witnessed at least one mental collapse at close quarters—and perhaps the most fascinating aspect of Waters's new lyrics was the implied presence of Syd Barrett. On a general level, he surely informed Waters's idea of a cold, acquisitive society stymying the potential of the individual, to the point that someone of a sensitive disposition might crack—but there were also more pointed references to his departed colleague. The chief example was a song that seems to have acted as the spark for Waters's whole concept: "Brain Damage," started by Waters toward the end of the sessions for *Meddle* and clearly inspired by John

[2] Waters's disdain for Mary Whitehouse later gave rise to a specific reference in "Pigs (Three Different Ones)" from 1997's *Animals:* "Hey you, Whitehouse … You house-proud town mouse … You gotta stem the evil tide." She died in 2001, aged ninety-one.

Dark Side's conceptualist-in-chief, backstage at Brighton Dome, January 1972. "I did feel at times close to madness myself." (Jill Furmanovsky)

Lennon's "Dear Prudence."

Its opening lines combined allusions to Barrett with a telling reference to Waters's youth in Cambridge. "In the first verse of 'Brain Damage,'" he says, "the grass that I talk about is the square of grass between King's College Chapel and the river.

I can see it in my mind very vividly." As with many of the city's gardens, this one has long been peppered with very English "Keep off the grass" notices; in Waters's lyric, sly tribute is perhaps paid to Barrett's singular, authority-defying mind in the line "the lunatic is on the grass" (its druggy connotations seem to have been accidental). More pointedly, there are lines whose references to Barrett are absolutely transparent: "If the dam breaks open, many years too soon"; "If the band you're in starts playing different tunes."

"There *was* a residue of Syd in all of this," says Waters. "It was pretty recent history. Syd had been the central creative force in the early days—maybe I provided some of the engine room—and so his having succumbed to schizophrenia was an enormous blow. And also, when you see that happening to someone you've been very close friends with, and known more or less your whole life, it really concentrates the mind on how ephemeral one's sensibilities and mental capacities can be. For me, it was very much 'There but for the grace of God go I.' That was certainly expressed in 'Brain Damage': the sense that one is not necessarily the master of one's own identity; that we're all marionettes, and the strings of our lives are pulled by our history, our backgrounds, our parents, our ancestors, and so on.

"I did feel at times close to madness myself. I can remember being in the canteen at Abbey Road, sitting at the table with everybody, and suddenly there was no pain; everything—the table, all the people at it—receded. The sound became tinny, and the room looked like I was looking at something through the wrong end of a pair of binoculars. I thought to myself, 'Wooah—hold a minute.' I hadn't been taking any drugs or anything. I thought, 'Wow—this is what it's like to go mad.' I clearly remember thinking that. And I got up from the table and resisted it. I walked up the stairs and went into studio number three and started playing the piano, and slowly things started to come back into a more normal perspective. It didn't happen again, but I was quite clear at the time that this was the beginning of a breakdown. It was a breakdown I resisted and never actually had."

Within "Brain Damage," Waters was clearly paying an emotive tribute to Barrett, though the lyrics—along with much of the new song cycle's themes—also chimed with a more intellectual take on his ex-colleague's predicament. In his own reductive way, Waters seemed to be drawing on the work of R. D. Laing, the "anti-psychiatrist," who had come close to treating Barrett in 1967. The sentiments expressed about madness in "Brain Damage" are of a piece with Laing's work; so too are Waters's later pronouncements about the notion of a "gestalt being" whose innocence is compromised and twisted by the adult world. "From the moment of birth," Laing wrote in 1967's *The Politics of Experience,* "when the stone-age baby confronts the twentieth-century mother, the baby is subjected to these forces of violence, called love, as its mother and father have been … these forces are mainly concerned with destroying most of its potentialities. This enterprise is on the whole successful." It may or not be a coincidence that one chapter of the same book is titled "Us and Them," which sets out much the same concerns as that song's first verse: "The brotherhood of man is evoked by particular men according to their circumstances. But it seldom extends to all men. In the name of our freedom and brotherhood we are prepared to blow up the other half of mankind and to be blown up in our turn."

Though such influences could easily have led to something that was florid, overwrought, and wide open to accusations of pretension—an accusation that could certainly be thrown at some of Waters's later work—

R. D. Laing, the "anti-psychiatrist" whose influence can be heard in "Us and Them" and "Brain Damage." "There were a whole team of them who all believed it was rather good to be mad." (Getty Images)

Waters was canny enough to ensure that his new songs' vocabulary was purposely accessible. Even within their most recent lyrics, the Floyd's roots in English psychedelia had still been evident—the Barrett-esque aspects of "Echoes" are a perfect case in point—but now they were set on a rather more straightforward course. "I think we all thought—and Roger definitely thought—that a lot of the lyrics that we had been using were a little too indirect," says David Gilmour. "There was definitely a feeling that the words were going to be very clear and specific. That was a leap forward. Things would mean what they meant. That was a distinct step away from what we had done before."

Gilmour's explanation reflects one of Floyd lore's most recurrent hallmarks: a view in which the band's development is seen largely on its own terms, and each successive album reflects a reaction to the band's past. It's a view only hardened by the common idea of Pink Floyd as a kind of sealed-off, self-sufficient entity that paid very little mind to outside developments. In fact, they were as open to contemporary influence as most of their peers—as proved by the line that can easily be drawn from Pink Floyd circa 1971–72 to the first solo work of one of Waters's heroes: John Lennon. Waters had already served notice of his inspirational debt in "Echoes": the words "Inviting and inciting me to rise" were a direct lift from the Beatles' "Across the Universe." Now, he based at least some of his quest to strip back his lyrics on *John Lennon/Plastic Ono Band,* the confessional, remarkably austere album that the ex-Beatle had released in late 1970. "I just think that's one of the truly great moments in the history of rock 'n' roll, or the history of any writing," says Waters. "It's a remarkable piece of work. It's so *raw.*"

Nonetheless, in his quest to push the Floyd's aesthetic somewhere new, Waters was also partly defining himself against the band's history—and the Syd Barrett period in particular. Given Waters's authorship of "Set the Controls for the Heart of the Sun," and his one-time desire to soundtrack sci-fi movies, the following words might seem rather disingenuous, but they give a flavor of his mindset at the start of work on *The Dark Side of the Moon:* "That was always my big fight in Pink Floyd: to try and drag it, kicking and screaming, back from the borders of space, from the whimsy that Syd was into—as beautiful as it is, into my concerns, which were much more political, and philosophical. Even now, people talk about space. What the fuck is that? None of it had anything to do with that. I don't know what's wrong with people. Space—what the fuck are they talking about? Inner space, maybe. I made a conscious effort when I was writing the lyrics for *Dark Side of the Moon* to take the enormous risk of being truly banal about a lot of it, in order that the ideas should be expressed as simply and plainly as possible."

This, inevitably, brought its own risks. "If you write 'Breathe, breathe in the air/Don't be afraid to care,' you leave yourself open to howling derision," says Waters. "People just go, 'You fucking wanker! How pathetic is that?' It's very adolescent in its intensity, but I'm very happy now that I took that risk."

The new song cycle initially took its name from the conclusive line of "Brain Damage." *The Dark Side of the Moon* seemed perfect, not only because of its aura of gravitas, but also on account of its crystallization of some of Waters's key themes. "When I say, 'I'll see you on the dark side of the moon,'" he later remarked, "what I mean ... is, 'If you feel that you're the only one ... that you seem crazy, 'cos you think everything is crazy, you're not alone.'" There was, however, one problem: the British blues-rock band Medicine Head was about to release an album called *Dark Side of the Moon.* Pink Floyd's new work was thus readied for its public premiere with the title *Eclipse,* and—in keeping with the elements that dealt with madness —subtitled "A piece for assorted lunatics."

Its opening run of performances, on a British tour that commenced on January 20, 1972, was clearly intended to decisively raise the technical standards of the band's shows. No less than nine tons of equipment—

including a twenty-eight-channel mixing desk, and quadraphonic sound system, intended to go beyond even the famed Azimuth Coordinator— were assembled, along with three huge trucks, and a tighty trained inner road crew numbering seven. As part of the package, the band commissioned a custom-built lighting rig (their first since 1968), intended to bolster the musical aspect of the show with unprecedented visual effects.

In a modern context, the idea of a group taking to the road to preview forty minutes of new material that would not be released for over a year might seem rather bizarre. In the U.K., however, Pink Floyd was a revered mainstay of a subculture—born in the 1960s and fixed as a key musical subculture by the start of the next decade—in which shows were often accorded the quiet respect that greets classical recitals. The contrast with their early experiences on the British ballroom circuit could not have been more pronounced: now, any idea of the rock gig as a hedonistic, noisy mass experience took second place to the importance of quietly *listening* (a process often assisted, it has to be said, by the sharing of the odd fragrant hand-rolled cigarette).

The human bedrock of all this was crowds of music-obsessed young men, whose identifying features were neatly summed by one British musician as follows: "Greatcoat, pint [of beer], album under your arm, sitting on the floor." The band's slowly growing American audiences were, needless to say, not all that different: certainly, U.S. concert tapes from the time suggest a similar atmosphere of hushed reverence. In that kind of context, the Floyd could be assured that being present for the premiere of their new music would be viewed as positive privilege.

By way of final preparation for the British tour, the group moved into a property owned by the Rolling Stones, in Bermondsey, South London—in Gilmour's recollection, "a dingy warehouse with a rehearsal room in it." Final run-throughs were subsequently staged at the Rainbow, a 5,000-capacity venue in the north of the city. Aside from simple matter of new songs and arrangements, the band also had to familiarize itself with new audio effects—among them, a tape loop that ran under the band's perform-ance of "Money," and a spoken-word addition to Rick Wright's "Mortality Sequence," built around excerpts from St. Paul's Letter to the Ephesians, and an appropriated monologue by Malcolm Muggeridge, a seventy-year-old socialist-turned-devout-Christian who had played a leading role in the Festival of Light, that moralistic Christian event that Waters had so despised.

A number of accounts of the period—not least Nick Mason's memoir *Inside Out*—date the public premiere of the new work to a run of shows in London that began on February 17. In fact, the new song cycle—along with such established pieces as "One of These Days," "Echoes," "Careful with That Axe Eugene," and "Set the Controls for the Heart of the Sun"—was first played on a run of English dates that included Coventry, Bristol, Manchester, and Liverpool, and began on January 20 in the coastal town of Brighton. The first show, unfortunately, did not quite count as *Eclipse*'s opening night: twenty-six minutes into the show, as the band clumsily attempted to keep time with the backing tape of "Money," an electrical fault caused everything to suddenly come to a halt. This part of the show

did not resume: panicked, the band quickly decided to replace "Eclipse" with "Atom Heart Mother," meaning that their work-in-progress was unveiled in its entirety the next night, along the South English coast in Portsmouth.

A tape exists of the Brighton performance, clearly sourced from within the audience. It begins with the all too familiar simulated heartbeat, occasionally accompanied by atonal keyboard swells, the odd taped sound effect—most noticeably, the cash-tills tape loop from "Money"—and the kind of audience reaction that speaks volumes about the band's new

Waters bangs the gong in Brighton,
where *Dark Side*'s premiere was cut
short by malfunctioning backing tapes.
(Jill Furmanovsky)

lighting effects. "Really great," enthuses one voice. "Look at that! Brilliant. *Jesus!*" Come the arrival of the songs, one thing becomes all too clear: a great deal of what we now know as *The Dark Side of the Moon* was in place, but it was still some distance from full realization. Relative to the album (and, indeed, later performances) the five pieces delivered in Brighton seem wildly uneven, ill-advisedly paced—and rather sullied by the fact that the band is still getting to grips with them.

"Breathe" arrives after two and a half minutes. The gentle ease of the recorded version sounds as if it's within the Floyd's grasp, but here the fluidity of the song is rather compromised by Gilmour marking the passage between the chords in the verse with a slightly clumsy ascending riff, clearly designed to ape the early section of "Echoes." The rather gauche air of the performance is only furthered by the vocal line: as against the grace and authority of the double-tracked self-duet he would eventually put to tape, he delivers the whole song in a hesitant semi-bellow, often sounding all but lost in the surrounding musical scenery.

And then the listener collides with the early *Dark Side*'s key glitch: the so-called Travel Section. Given that the song cycle has barely started, bridging the gap between "Breathe" and "Time" with a seven-minute improvisation, largely bounced between Gilmour and Rick Wright, represents a pretty off-beam sense of dynamics—an impression that hardens into concrete certainty at around its fifth minute. Descending chordal guitar runs endlessly collide with Wright's jazz-inspired keyboard trills—redolent, for better or worse, of the Doors' Ray Manzarek circa *LA Woman*—while Nick Mason bravely attempts to infuse the resultant mess with some sense of momentum. If it was meant to evoke "some kind of crash," it was certainly overlong; as to give the band a hint that things have misfired, the audience greets its eventual conclusion—a slow passage into inconclusive half-silence—with no audible applause.

"Time," mercifully, fares a little better. Certainly, its two bridge sections —marked by Rick Wright's lead vocal—give notice of the wonders to

93

come, though in its early form, it still comes out sounding uncomfortably underwhelming. There is one particular problem: the taut, funked-up dynamics that defined the recorded version's verses are nowhere to be heard. Instead, Gilmour and Wright—dueting on the verses—sing Waters's words with a fatalistic, wearied quality that reflects the song's sentiments but leaves the music feeling rather flat. Compounding such difficulties, both vocalists recurrently forget the words.

That song, after the brief reprise of "Breathe," gives way to Rick Wright's "Mortality Sequence": a four-and-a-half-minute mélange of a churchy organ part and spoken-word sound effects that develops the last few lines of the previous piece, and their evocation of the church bell calling "the faithful to their knees." On *The Dark Side of the Moon,* such images are quickly pushed to one side by "The Great Gig in the Sky"; here, the band clearly attempts to make some kind of diffuse comment on Christianity, replete with fragments of prayers ("By our father, we confess to thee/We confess to thee with our whole heart"), biblical excerpts, and the aforementioned clips of Malcolm Muggeridge, apparently paying tribute to the public's response to his religious campaigning: "I only wish I could show you the number of letters of support which I have received." By its close, the music has been swamped by a kind of pious cacophony, before an electronic buzz cuts through the sound, and we hear the seven-to-the-bar tape loop that begins "Money."

In the overlap of Wright's organ and the sound of cash registers and falling coins, the Floyd may have been nodding to a skeptical and very English view of Sunday morning ritual, in which every visit to church eventually sees the circulation of the dreaded Collection Box—but any such point was soon lost in the midst of an unfortunate mishap. "Money" begins with Waters's clunkily delivered bass-line: a plodding, singularly non-groovy sound, made all the more unsatisfactory by the absence of the subtle Gilmour guitar figure that initially shadows it on the album. His colleagues eventually crash in, at first playing faster than the tape, and awkwardly setting into a meter that rather suggests a stilted kind of march-time. After a little over twenty bars, the group stutters into chaos; two rapid-fire drum shots and a cymbal splash from Nick Mason signal that things have gone sufficiently awry that they can only draw matters to halt. After twenty-two seconds that feel more like a matter of minutes, the audience offers the group a spurt of encouraging, charitable applause.

On the tape, two more minutes go by, punctuated by the recording stopping and starting, until Roger Waters comes to the microphone. "That was a pity," he deadpans.

Another couple of minutes passes, before the recording comes back to life with another burst of applause, and the sound of the band tuning up. "Okay," says Waters. "Due to severe mechanical and electronic horror, we shan't do any more of that bit, so we'll do something else." The version of "Atom Heart Mother" that follows is almost unbearably weary: the sound, perhaps, of a band reluctantly going back to music they had assumed they were well on the way to leaving to history.

Thankfully, the next seven shows—in Portsmouth, Bournemouth, Southampton, Newcastle, Leeds, Coventry, and Bristol—saw "Eclipse" delivered in its entirety. On the latter date, moreover, it took another small step toward its full realization when Roger Waters, in the wake of a day off on February 4, presented the group with the song cycle's hastily written epilogue, which served—for now, anyway—as its title track. "I think I arrived at the gig with the song in my pocket," he says. "I said something like, 'Here lads, I've written the ending.'"

Largely sung by Waters alone, "Eclipse" was a two-minute, 6/8 creation, seemingly tied into the elements of the new music that dealt with death, in which a list of life's key experiences ("All that you touch/And all that you see") climaxed with the evocation of the moon eclipsing the sun. With "Brain Damage" as the finale, things had ended on a note of empathetic warmth; now, Waters had apparently come up with a far bleaker conclusion—though he has long claimed that his intentions were altogether more benign. "In a strange way," he later commented, "it reattached me to my adolescence [and] the dreams of youth…. It's a *recitatif* of the ideas that preceded it—saying, 'There you are, that's all there is to it: What you experience is what it [i.e. life] is.' The rather depressing ending, 'And everything under the sun is in tune/but the sun is eclipsed by the moon,' is the idea we all have the potential to be in harmony … to lead happy, meaningful, and right lives."

Given the cancellation of the next day's show in Plymouth, this new piece was worked up and added to "Eclipse," receiving its debut at Leicester's De Montfort Hall on February 10. One week later, the Floyd reached London, for four nights at the Rainbow Theatre, during which the U.K. music press were in attendance en masse, along with the odd bootlegger: in time, around 120,000 copies of the illicit London recordings were sold to the more hardcore elements of the band's public.

As evidenced by one such tape—a soundboard recording, dated to the last night of the four London shows—many of the problems in Brighton were still evident, particularly the directionless, momentum-sapping nature of "The Travel Section" and Rick Wright's "Mortality Sequence" (for "Money," the troublesome loops were faded down as soon as the whole band began playing). All that said, *The Dark Side of the Moon* was starting to audibly cohere. "Breathe" is delivered with a serene ease that speaks volumes about the group's snowballing confidence. When "Money" snaps into its frantic 4/4 middle section, the group—led, of course, by David Gilmour—achieves a thrilling power and drive. "Brain Damage," in its own way, may be the most impressive piece on the tape: Roger Waters's fragile vocals suit the song's sentiments to perfection, and its segued transition of "Eclipse" is simply delightful. Tellingly, the end of that song is followed by thirty seconds of frantic applause.

By and large, the assembled journalists were as enthused as the rest of the audience, though their interpretations of Waters's thematic conceit were amusingly varied. For *NME, The Dark Side of the Moon* was "an assault on the corruption of media—delivered, ironically enough, with all the facilities of media at their disposal: gigantic light-towers, banks of quadraphonic speakers, taped harangues from Muggeridge and his ilk; all swirling, floating and moving from space to space, leaving the listeners stunned and yet not bewildered." The writer went on: "At the end of the piece, police sirens echoed through the Rainbow ... and the main light-tower—to the accompaniment of agonised mechanical groans—dipped in mock-salute to media, to the Floyd and to us. Tremendous."

Melody Maker, unfortunately, rather lazily went back to the sci-fi clichés of the recent past. *Dark Side,* they claimed, was "a kind of space fantasy opera, where the all-round speaker system, pre-recorded tapes (including Muggeridge's voice), and spectacular lighting columns play as big a part as the instrumental work onstage." Their reporter's conclusion suggested that for all the Rainbow crowd's rapture, there were some people who were probably never going to get it: "Musically, there were some great ideas, but the sound effects often let me wondering if I was in a bird-cage at London zoo."

The review that came closest to grasping the band's intentions came from the august, upmarket *Sunday Times.* "It looks like hell," wrote one Derek Jewell. "The set is dominated by three silver towers of light that hiccough eerie shades of red, green and blue cross the stage. Smoke haze from blinding flares that have erupted and died drifts everywhere ... If all this sounds like [Dante's] *The Inferno* reworked, you would be only partly right. The ambition of the Floyd's artistic intention is now vast." He went on to pay empathetic tribute to "an uncanny feeling for the melancholy of our time," concluding that, "In their own terms, Floyd strikingly succeed. They are dramatists supreme."

Three days after the last of the London shows, Pink Floyd were across the English Channel, beginning a week's stay at Chateau D'Herouville, the

RAINBOW THEATRE
(ASTORIA)
FINSBURY PARK :: LONDON

THE PINK FLOYD
EVENING 8-0
THURSDAY
FEBRUARY **17**
CIRCLE
£1·00
Block I
Q37
FOR CONDITIONS OF SALE SEE OVER
THIS PORTION TO BE RETAINED

(oppposite) The Rainbow, London, February 1972. "The ambition of the Floyd's artistic intention is now vast," raved one critic. (Jill Furmanovsky)

(Ticket stub courtesy of Ian Russell)

(left) Wright and Waters with engineer Roger Quested, working on final over-dubs for *Obscured by Clouds.* "We sat in a room, and wrote and recorded like a production line." (Nick Mason's Archive)

French residential studio to which Elton John paid tribute in the title of *Honky Chateau,* the album put to tape there mere weeks before the Floyd's arrival. They were there at the behest of Barbet Schroeder, the director who had employed them to record the soundtrack to 1969's *More;* this time, they were charged with responsibility of coming up with a score for *La Vallée,* another rather stereotypical counterculture movie involving the attempts of a gaggle of French hippies to find a higher truth on an adventure in Papua New Guinea. "We sat in a room, and wrote and recorded like a production line," said Dave Gilmour. "Very good to work like that sometimes—under extreme constraints of time and trying to meet someone else's needs."

The resultant album, though hardly among the band's most important records, amounts to much more than a mere footnote. Taken on its own, it's a subtly accomplished collection of music, in which the Floyd occasionally reveal sides of themselves that do not quite fit with their art-rock stereotype—as in the Wright/Waters collaboration "Stay," an airbrushed bit of mainstream balladry that forgoes anything experimental in favor of a straight-laced love song; and "The Gold It's in the …," for which the band dispenses a strain of gonzo blues-rock (a close relative, it has to be said, of the Small Faces' 1969 single "Wham Bam Thank You Mam"[3]) that sounds so out of character as to be almost hilarious—not least when Dave Gilmour attempts to bend his polite English vocal into American-flavored raunch.

In the context of *The Dark Side of the Moon,* some of the music forms a neat set of companion pieces. There are hints of the songs they had been playing in concert for the previous month: Gilmour's delicate slide guitar on "Burning Bridges"; the serene feel—à la "Breathe" and "Us and Them"—of "Mudmen"; the sharpened, steely aspects of Gilmour's "Childhood's End" that presage the eventual treatment given to the verses of "Time." Perhaps most insightful, however, is Waters's solo composition "Free Four": on the face of it way too whimsical to be considered of a piece with any of *Dark Side,* and yet built from the kind of themes that he had tapped into for what was still known as "Eclipse." Its first and second verses, for all the camped-up joviality of the music, tap into the same ideas as "Time": "Life is a short warm moment … you get your chance to try, in the twinkling of an eye." The next stanza finds the narrator bemoaning the advent of yet another American tour, before the song approaches its end via an elliptical reference to Eric Fletcher Waters. Had its author thought to develop the song further—a chorus, for example, might have been an idea—it could have numbered among the best things he had written thus far; completely unexpectedly, it was eventually championed by American

---

[3] There is at least one more specific link between the two bands within the small print of Pink Floyd history: Seamus, the dog who can be heard barking on the track of the same name from *Meddle,* belonged to the ex–Small Faces vocalist Steve Marriott.

FM radio, thus propelling the album—released in June 1972 as *Obscured by Clouds*—into the U.S. top 50, hitherto virgin territory for its authors.

In the meantime, Pink Floyd bowed to the inevitable and carried on touring. In early March, "Eclipse"—along with such standard supporting features as "Echoes" and "Careful with That Axe Eugene"—was played to Japanese audiences in Tokyo, Osaka, Kyoto, and Sapporo. By the middle of April, the band had begun a fifteen-date U.S. tour that climaxed with two shows at New York's Carnegie Hall. May saw three gigs in Germany and the Netherlands—the latter two of which, for some reason, saw "Eclipse" dropped in favor of "Atom Heart Mother"—before the group finally came home on May 23. They were not due to play another show for a month. Wasting no time, Pink Floyd was about to finally go back into the studio.

4

FORWARD, HE CRIED FROM THE REAR: INTO ABBEY ROAD

"We always seemed to be doing records in the middle of other things," says Dave Gilmour. "We'd work for three days, and then we'd go and do a gig in Belgium, and then we'd do three days in Paris, and go back into the studio a month later. It seemed completely normal."

"It was different then," says Nick Mason. "You didn't do world tours; you went and did Germany, and then you did Holland, and then you came back home. We tended not to want to tour for very long periods anyway, but also, we weren't of a stature to be heading off on world tours. The setup costs for touring were entirely different: you go on a world tour now for two years, and it'll take you six months to get the setup costs back, because you've built a stage, and a screen, and a thing that revolves, and another thing that comes out of the ground, and you've got a lighting truss that weighs 100 tons ... you *have* to do it like that. Then, we would never have dreamt of doing it that way."

Thanks to Pink Floyd's stop-start touring schedule, though the *The Dark Side of the Moon* sessions took up around forty days, they were spread over the next seven months. The first stint at Abbey Road began at the end of May 1972: a total of eighteen days, leading up to a handful of live commitments in France and Britain. Thankfully, if the group hardly seemed to mind the obligation to recurrently head out on the road, the key people with whom they worked on *Dark Side* seemed to feel much the same way. "I think it was healthy," says Alan Parsons, whose minor legend was forged thanks to his work as the album's recording engineer. "I'm not one for spending eternal weeks on end, concentrating on getting something finished. I think it was beneficial to get away from it now and again. And for the band to go through the experience of playing the music live was very healthy."

In June 1972, Parsons was twenty-three years old. His résumé was inevitably brief, but undoubtedly impressive: having first found employment at an EMI tape duplication plant, he had quickly joined the staff of Abbey Road, working as an assistant engineer on the Beatles' *Abbey Road*, and rising to take the senior engineer role on parts of Paul McCartney's inaugural solo work, McCartney and Wings' debut album *Wild Life*. Along the way, he had fleetingly assisted in the recording of both *Ummagumma* and *Atom Heart Mother*. His impressive track record, however, was not reflected in his salary: in return for his services, Parsons was paid £35 (around $60) a week.

Compared to his experiences with the Floyd in the recent past, Parsons quickly realized that the new sessions represented a new way of working. "The key thing that was different," he says, "was that they had a piece of music they'd been playing live, so it had structure. *Atom Heart Mother* had had a little bit of structure when it arrived, but *Dark Side of the Moon* was a fait accompli. It was very structured, *together*. They didn't have to mess around with the compositions, although they did develop naturally through the recording process. The songs were there."

In truth, however, even if the band had reverted to the procrastinating behavior of yore, Parsons would still have been thrilled to be sharing their company. "The Floyd were, by their very nature, audio experimentalists," he says enthusiastically. "And to be the engineer with that kind of outfit was a dream come true. The Beatles were the only band who had done that. Not only did the Floyd have the inclination to spend large amounts of time experimenting with sound, but they had the time, and the record company had the budget. The Floyd and the Beatles have a lot in common in that respect—and they both worked in the greatest studios with some of the greatest engineers.

"There's no question of that," he says. "And I'm not just blowing my own trumpet in relation to *The Dark Side of the Moon;* that goes for a lot of records that they made. We were a good team; we worked well together." (In their own way, the band concurs with all this: "EMI was a great place to work," says Nick Mason. "There were a lot of people with good ideas there, who'd make things work—a lot of 'Well, let's try this.'")

Whereas *Meddle* had been put to tape in a variety of London studios, the new album would be recorded exclusively in Abbey Road, belatedly equipped with the sixteen-track equipment that had been lacking in 1971. Nonetheless, the Floyd's new music was sufficiently ambitious to rub up against even these dizzying new limits. "It was better than eight-track," says Parsons, "but you had to think carefully about how many layers you could physically achieve; you couldn't just add and add and add like you would now. And we did get to the stage where we pretty much filled up the tape on most of the songs, and we decided to go to a second generation and reduce the sixteen tracks down to seven or eight, so we had more space for overdubs. The downside of that was that the second-generation tape lost quality. We lost a bit in the mixdown process."

In the recollections of Parsons and the band, live performances were not the only reason for recording frequently being drawn to a close. Roger Waters's love of soccer was certainly allowed to take precedence over work at Abbey Road: as a passionate fan of the London team Arsenal, which had won both the English league and FA cup (English soccer's equivalent of the

Superbowl) in 1971, he would regularly break from recording and head to their home ground in North London, not far from his home. "I used to literally dream of playing for Arsenal in those days," Waters says. "I lived in the New North Road in Islington from 1968 until 1975. And I went to see Arsenal for every home game when I was in London. I was deeply engrossed in the idea of football teams. You can hear some of that in 'Money': 'Think I'll buy me a football team' …"

"The hours we worked depended on which day of the week it was," says Parsons. "If it was football [i.e. soccer] night, we would always finish early; Roger was *very* into any big matches that were going on at the time. He was into playing it as well. There was a Pink Floyd team. And if *Monty Python* was on TV we'd do the same: very often, we'd stop for *Monty Python* and they would leave me to do a rough mix of the story so far, so they could assess what they'd done. That was quite fulfilling for me. I got to put my own mark on what we were doing."

When they were in the studio, Parsons— like so many of the Floyd's assistants and collaborators—quickly noticed one of the band's most remarkable attributes: its very English sense of reserve and understatement. These were not the kind of musicians, it became clear, who would celebrate a successful take with the massed cheers and the popping of corks. "It was all very calm; very unenthusiastic," he says. "They would never be jumping up and down with joy when something was working. After an amazing take on a guitar solo, Roger would say something like, 'Oh, I think we might be able to get away with that one, Dave.' It was really very low-key."

(above) Alan Parsons, the engineer whose labors on *Dark Side* earned him around $60 a week. "Very often, we'd stop for *Monty Python* and they would leave me to do a rough mix." (Nick Mason's Archive)

(opposite) Pink Floyd pictured in Abbey Road's canteen. "It was all very calm. They would never be jumping up and down with joy." (Taken from the DVD *Live at Pompeii: The Director's Cut*)

All that said, the first phase of the Abbey Road sessions saw at least one member of the group break from the group's usually taciturn behavior: Nick Mason, who was perhaps exhibiting symptoms of the recurrent Floyd disease whereby—to use his own phrase—"getting started was always the problem."

"The first week was almost disastrous," says Parsons. "Nick Mason just wasn't happy with his drum sound. Whether he felt that in order to get the best result we needed to spend a lot of time on the drums, I don't know … but whatever it was, we got over it. As we got into the fourth or fifth week of recording tracks, he didn't even bother to go through the process of checking the drum sound. We would just do it, and that would be it. The feeling of trust between us all improved as time went on."

All told, the young engineer seemed to be performing a delicate balancing act, ensuring that he made no attempt to intrude on the band's well-tested processes of decision-making, but occasionally taking the initiative and thereby laying claim to a more creative role than his job title might have suggested. "I just acted on instincts. I didn't thrust my ideas at them: I would occasionally make suggestions, and occasionally do things I felt were right without asking."

Soon enough, says Parsons, he began to feel tightly tied in to the work they were putting to tape. "The thing was, we all knew that this was something more carefully crafted than anything they'd done before: something very, very special."

The first song the band began was "Us and Them," whose core elements—bass, drums, piano, organ, guitar, along with Rick Wright and David Gilmour's vocals—were recorded from June 1 onwards. Six days later, they started work on "Money," the song whose live performances had been bolstered—and, initially at least, bedeviled—by the seven-beat sound-effects loop that had been enterprisingly manufactured by Roger Waters.

"I made those recordings in a shed at the bottom of the garden, throwing coins into a big industrial food-mixing bowl that my wife used for mixing clay," says Waters. "I recorded the sound effects on my first proper tape recorder, chopped them up and glued them together, stuck them in the machine, put a mic stand up to hold the tape taut and it went [impersonates effects]."

When it came to recording in Abbey Road, however, the band's technological aspirations meant that the loop had to be re-recorded. The album, they had decided, was to be released not only in conventional stereo, but also in quadraphonic—that stereotypically '70s invention whereby audiophiles could place a speaker on each wall of a room, and allegedly luxuriate in the closest available thing to surround-sound.[4]

"Because it was designed for quadraphonic," explains Alan Parsons, "instead of being on quarter-inch tape, the 'Money' effects had to be on a one-inch loop, with all the sounds recorded on different tracks. The idea was that when the record was played, the sounds would go around the room. Length-wise, each of the sounds lasted about a second—which is about fifteen inches of tape. Times that by seven, and you've got quite a big length of tape. And that had to be routed around a few obstacles in the studio.

"It would be remarkably easy now: you could do it in about fifteen minutes," he continues. "But we had to record the sounds individually. Some of them, like the cash register, came from sound effects records that were lurking in the Abbey Road tape library. One of the sounds is something called a Uni-selector, which you'd find in a telephone exchange: that's the 'Brrrr' kind of sound, the third before last. And we got bags of cash and recorded them being dropped from a height of six feet on the studio floor. There was another sound that was meant to represent money being torn up: that was just bits of paper. The Floyd weren't that rich then."

"With the tape loops on 'Money,' we had mic stands set up in the control room, with yards of tape doing a circle," says Gilmour. "But you had to keep it tight enough, because otherwise it would get screwed up in the tape machine—so it was zooming around all these mic stands. Everything that

---

[4] A quadraphonic version of *The Dark Side of the Moon*, mixed by Alan Parsons, was released not long after the conventional stereo version of the album, only to be eventually deleted. "Quadraphonic sound died a horrible death," says Parsons. "Nobody believed in it; it really wasn't very good. The hardware didn't really work, and black vinyl wasn't robust enough to carry it."

one can do these days digitally, in seconds, was a major logistical night-mare. We were all experts in cutting and splicing tape and making loops, because we had to be."

Aside from the effects—as on the Rainbow tape, they were faded out inside a few bars of the song's opening—"Money" was also remarkable because of the band's attempt to push themselves into the kind of groove-laden music that had reared its head during "Echoes" and "Atom Heart Mother." This time, however, their ideas were a little more developed: as well as Waters's strident main riff, the verses of the song were partly propelled by the interplay between Rick Wright's electric piano, and sharp stabs of funk-flavored guitar played by Dave Gilmour. In addition, the 4/4 segment during which Gilmour delivered an improvised solo (subsequently learned by rote and faithfully delivered at the band's shows) betrayed the strong influence of the kind of American musicians they had held in high esteem during their youth.

"I was always trying to put a bit of that into things," says Gilmour. "I was constantly trying to get Nick to learn new drum patterns and get slightly funkier. Getting specific about how and what influenced what is always difficult, but I was a big Booker T fan. I had the *Green Onions* album when I was a teenager. And in my previous band [i.e. Jokers Wild], we were going for two or three years, and went through the Beatles and Beach Boys, on to all the Stax and soul stuff: things like Otis Redding. We played 'Green Onions' onstage. I'd done a fair bit of that stuff; it was some-thing I thought we could incorporate into our sound without anyone spot-ting where the influence had come from.

"To me," he says, "it worked. You could combine all this other stuff with that slightly more funky style. Nice white English architecture stu-dents getting funky is a bit of an odd thought." He laughs: "And isn't as funky as all that."

Certainly, if the band were aspiring to the kind of locked-tight groove one associates with the likes of the MGs, there was one glaring fault: their rather shaky sense of timekeeping. "The backing track was everyone playing together: a Wurlitzer piano through a wah-wah, bass, drums, and guitar," Roger Waters later remembered. "One of the ways you can tell that it was done live is that the tempo changes so much from the beginning to the end. It speeds up fantastically."

The next piece to be started was "Time," whose basic tracks were begun the day after work commenced on "Money." Now, the sense of lethargy that had held back its early live readings was gone: the verses—sung by a solo Gilmour in aggressive, gravelly tones that lay light-years from the hushed timbre he used on such songs as "Breathe" and "Us and Them"—crackled with an energy that exploded into the passage reserved for a guitar solo. "The guitar solos were all improvised," Alan Parsons later remembered. "Dave used to play at deafening volumes.... I would just use one microphone, about a foot away."

Gilmour was, and remains, a devout believer in the serendipitous magic of off-the-cuff invention. "You just go out and have a play over it and see what it becomes," he later reflected, "and usually it's the first take that's the best one."

Rick Wright, by contrast, had spent many hours perfecting the instrumental interlude that was still known variously as "The Mortality Sequence" and "The Religious Section." The organ piece that had been played at the early "Eclipse" shows, however, had been put to one side: instead, Wright had come up with a piece played on the piano that was a little more conventionally Floyd-esque, with room for drums, bass, and organ. By way of tying it into the music that surrounded it, the piece's most lengthy passage echoed "Breathe." Its switch between the chords of G minor 7 and C9 was subtly redolent of that song's E minor/A foundation, a point only underlined by a brief but gorgeous steel guitar part in its opening bars.

In turn, that section built up to a tumultuous crescendo, and then gave way to its most impressive passage: the period of portentous calm that arrived two-and-a-half minutes into the piece. If it was initially intended to evoke death, Wright has subsequently suggested that such thoughts were some distance from his mind: "When I wrote it, I didn't think, 'This is all about death'—because [if I had] I don't think I would have written that chord structure."

According to Alan Parsons, Wright put his part to tape in isolation from the rest of his colleagues. "Rick was in Number One studio, playing one of the big grand pianos, and the band were in Number Two studio," he says. "We played a trick on him: instead of the band actually playing, we played the previous take off a tape. There was no way Rick would have noticed the difference. So we ran the tape and sneaked into the doorway—and when he looked up at the end of the take, everyone was standing there, looking at him. He looked a little surprised. We were a bunch of kids really, playing pranks."

At that point, the piece was viewed as a success—"one of the best things Rick ever did," in Waters's estimation—though there seems to have also been a creeping suspicion that it was in need of an additional element. For the moment, the band provisionally stuck to the idea of accompanying Wright's music with the spoken-word tapes they had been using in concert. As an alternative, however, Alan Parsons grafted on a section from an archive NASA recording—only to find that the group, doubtless mindful of yet more sci-fi associations, were less than keen. "I put some dialogue from a space-walk on 'The Great Gig in the Sky,'" he recalls, "which I thought worked really well."

He allows himself a smirk. "And they didn't."

It was perhaps a sign of the Floyd's very English variety of cool-headedness that they made the most of the summer of 1972 by taking two months off. Their work in the studio was thus put on hold, while the band holidayed with their wives, girlfriends, and families—and quietly prepared for the U.S. tour that would begin that September.

It duly began with a low-key engagement at the Municipal Auditorium in Austin, Texas—a show that nonetheless marked a crucial point in the progress of the band's new song cycle. From here on in, the forty-odd minutes of music that they had been honing for ten months would be known as *The Dark Side of the Moon.* In Dave Gilmour's recollection, the threat from the Medicine Head album of the same name was deemed to have passed: "It didn't sell well, so what the hell.… I was against 'Eclipse' and we felt a bit annoyed because we'd already thought of the title before the Medicine Head record came out … we wanted to use it." For now, however, the old strap-line was still in place: Pink Floyd's *Dark Side* remained "a piece for assorted lunatics."

After Austin, the band called at cities including Tucson, Wichita, and Tempe—examples of what the record industry now terms "Secondary Markets"—before staging a fondly remembered spectacular at the Hollywood Bowl, the Californian holy-of-holies that, ever since the Beatles performed there in 1964, had stood as a byword for the ambitions of ascendant English rock groups. "In our pre–*Dark Side of the Moon* days, we were going through a gradual buildup of popularity in America," says Dave Gilmour, "and we were beginning to sell out quite large halls—12,000 seaters. And someone suggested that the Hollywood Bowl would be good fun, and it was. It was a fantastic night. We had those huge Hollywood spotlights outside: four of them, set a couple of hundred yards apart, creating a pyramid over the stage—and another swath of rainbow-colored lights, like a fan behind it. It knocked us all out."

The tour drew into its concluding run of dates in the Pacific Northwest, where the band played in Portland, Seattle, and Vancouver. In the latter city, the first of their performances at the Gardens Arena was reviewed by a correspondent from the avowedly countercultural *Vancouver Free Press,* who was impressed enough by the band's music, but deeply thrilled by both their light show, and the impact it had on certain members of the audience. "There was a lot of dope doing the rounds," he wrote, "and there were a few tripping initiates to Pink Floyd concerts that were heard giving wild shouts … the guy next to me shot bolt upright as if someone had cracked a whole cluster of amyl nitrates under his nostrils."

Ten days later, Pink Floyd arrived back at Abbey Road for the second spate of work on *The Dark Side of the Moon*. They had two broad objectives: to begin work on the songs that had failed to make it into the June sessions, and to start fine-tuning and filling out the pieces they had already put to tape. On the first count, they commenced the recording of "Brain Damage," "Eclipse," "Any Colour You Like," and "The Travel Section," soon to be known as "On the Run." By way of achieving the second aim, they brought in an admirable team of female vocalists, whose role could perhaps be traced to Waters and Ron Geesin's soundtrack to *The Body:* its finale, featuring all four members of the Floyd, had been a gently uplifting song entitled "Give Birth to a Smile" (whose bucolic, naturalistic imagery seems also to have set the tone for "Breathe"), bolstered by the unprecedented addition of soul-influenced backing singers.

In 1970s London, any rock artist in need of female vocal support—from ex-Beatles, through such freshly launched sensations as Queen and T-Rex, to visiting American musicians—tended to draw on a small circle of singers, numbering no more than ten. Given the breadth of their contribution to some of the most fondly loved records in the rock canon, the place of this tight-knit community in musical history has long been lamentably underrated. "We were all big mates," says Barry St. John, who—among her other appearances—numbered among the backing vocalists on records by Elton John, Rod Stewart, and Mott the Hoople (her real name was Eliza Thomson; the first half of her alias came from Barrie Chase, a sometime dance partner of Fred Astaire). "We all genuinely liked each other. We wouldn't just turn up to do a session and say, 'Right—see you then.' We actually talked to each other. A lot of us were working-class girls. We all stuck together and helped each other out."

St. John joined three other singers, assembled by the Floyd for an

(Opposite, clockwise from top left) Liza Strike, Barry St. John, Lesley Duncan, and Doris Troy, *Dark Side*'s backing vocalists. "The most we got was 'That'll do.' There were no smiles; we were all quite relieved to get out."(Redferns/Fin Costello)

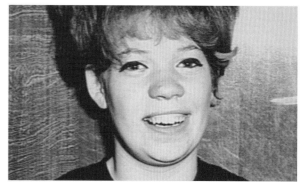

afternoon session at Abbey Road. Liza Strike had begun her session career by contributing to the 1970 solo album Stephen Stills recorded in London, and gone on to become one of the U.K.'s most ubiquitous session vocalists. Doris Troy (aka Doris Payne) was a New York–born soul and gospel singer who had settled in London and been briefly signed to the Beatles' Apple label. "Doris was a character," says Strike. "We lived round the corner from each other. She would call me up and say, 'Hey—you drivin' today, baby? Well, pick me up, baby.' She was very Harlem—she came from the rough side of New York, and she stayed that way. She was *big*."[5]

The foursome was completed by Lesley Duncan, a twenty-nine-year-old singer/songwriter and session vocalist whose chief claim to fame was "Love Song," a composition covered by Elton John on 1970's *Tumbleweed Connection*. She had also contributed vocals to such gargantuan British hits as the Love Affair's "Everlasting Love" and "Goo Goo Barabajagal (Love Is Hot)," the 1969 collaboration between Donovan and Jeff Beck.

In Duncan's recollection, the singers' visit to Abbey Road shone light on an amusing irony: though the band's new songs bemoaned humanity's lack of mutual understanding and emotional generosity, the Floyd outwardly seemed to be part of the problem. "They weren't very friendly," she says. "They were cold; rather clinical. They didn't emanate any kind of *warmth*. You'd normally have quite a nice time doing sessions with people —you didn't go to the pub or anything, but you'd usually have a bit of laugh, and there was a sense of everyone being in it together. It wasn't like that at all. They just said what they wanted and we did it. I have a very clear memory of standing in the control room, listening back to what we'd done, feeling this very chilly atmosphere and thinking, 'Have we done something wrong? They obviously don't like what we're doing.' The most we got was 'That'll do.' There were no smiles; we were all quite relieved to get out."

"It was very serious," says Liza Strike. "At lots of sessions, there were a few jokes going around. This was very quiet; there was no interchange

5 Doris Troy, Liza Strike, and Barry St. John's vocals can be heard on John Lennon's 1971 single "Power to the People."

between us as people. Dave Gilmour was running it, and he knew exactly what he wanted. We weren't referred to much. Even when I was ad-libbing, he told me what to sing. Usually, people would say 'Can you ad-lib there?' and leave it open. But he played what he wanted. "

The quartet's vocals were added to "Us and Them" (on which they were triple-tracked) and "Brain Damage," along with "Eclipse"—on which Troy and Strike delivered a brief series of wonderfully gospelized improvisations. They were perhaps put to most impressive use, however, on "Time," for which their vocals were eventually passed through a Frequency Translator, an early pitch-shifting device. The result was a glorious ambient wash that allowed the passages sung by Rick Wright to take on a grace that its live versions had hinted at but never quite achieved. "These inventions were never used in the way they were intended," Alan Parsons later said. "We made this discovery that if you fed it back into itself, it made this wonderful swishing noise."

The vocalists—listed on the track sheets as "girls"—were not the only extra addition to the music. On two of the songs put to tape back in June, the group decided to overdub sax parts—and rather than contacting a musician from the ranks of London's sessioneers, they put in a call to a friend from Cambridge. Dick Parry was a little older than the crowd who had gathered at the Criterion and formed the milieu from which half the Floyd had come, but he and David Gilmour were long-standing acquaintances.

"I had played with him," Gilmour recalled. "He was a jazz player. My

Saxophonist Dick Parry, called to Abbey Road thanks to his connections with David Gilmour. (Jill Furmanovsky)

group in Cambridge very rarely had a gig on a Sunday night, and Dick had a regular spot in a ballroom on that night. We got this jazz trio thing going on. Pink Floyd were so insular in some ways, thinking about it. We didn't know anyone; we really didn't know how to get hold of a sax player. We wanted to try a sax on 'Us and Them' and 'Money,' so we got Dick in."

Parry played two very different solos. For "Us and Them," Gilmour's suggested point of reference was the role played by Gerry Mulligan on *Gandharva,* a partly live album by the American electronic pioneers Paul Beaver and Bernie Krause that had been released the previous year. The result was a series of warm, gently melodic touches that bookended the verses, were used in the choruses, and were allowed to drift over an instrumental passage before the last vocal stanzas (on early takes, they were scattered far wider, punctuating just about all the phrases). "Money," meanwhile, found Parry delivering an altogether more forceful contribution, in keeping with Gilmour's wish to approximate his favorite R'n'B musicians.

Finally, it was around this same time that a new element was spliced onto the intro of "Time": a volley of clocks, recently recorded by Alan Parsons for an EMI record aimed at demonstrating the wonders of quadraphonic sound. After a barrage of ticking sounds, the band wanted Parsons's various chimes and alarms to sound simultaneously; so it was that the recording studio was once again festooned with lengths of tape, while the Floyd and their accomplices managed yet another small feat of ingenuity.

Soon enough, Pink Floyd were back on tour: this time, playing *The Dark Side of the Moon* to a run of audiences in mainland Europe. They began in Copenhagen, before traveling south and stopping in the German cities of Hamburg, Dusseldorf, and Frankfurt—and Boblingen, a suburb of Stuttgart that was the home to an indoor arena known as the Sporthalle.

A bootleg tape of the latter show finds the band relaxing into *Dark Side* as never before, betraying their deep familiarity with the material by frequently adding ad hoc touches, at least some of which were improvised on the spot. The intro of "Breathe" features an unexpected Gilmour guitar solo. "The Travel Section," still played according to the guitar-jam model, finds Roger Waters falling into the three-note bass riff that underpinned both "Let There Be More Light" from *A Saucerful of Secrets* and the middle passage of "Interstellar Overdrive"; stranger still, it concludes with a brief boogie-rock passage. Oddest of all, however, is an extended rendition of "Any Colour You Like," during which Gilmour temporarily reinvents himself as the Floyd's answer to George Benson, and showily sings along to his guitar parts. The idea was retained on early studio takes of the song—a track was set aside for vocals, and its working title was "Scat"—but is mercifully undetectable on the released version.

Other aspects of the tape prove that *Dark Side* was still very much a work in progress. The lyrics of "Time" still feature the line "Lying supine in the sunshine," later amended to "tired of lying in the sunshine." "The Great Gig in the Sky" is radically different from the finished version: the cacophony of Christian voices is still in place, and the passage in which the whole band crashes in is hampered by a hideously clumsy Waters bass line, in which he plunks upward through the most rudimentary of scales. In "Us and Them," meanwhile, the conclusion of each verse is marked by Gilmour issuing a valedictory and uncomfortably corny "Aaaah"—a touch that would be sensibly dropped by the time *Dark Side* was completed.

Five days later, the group unveiled one of their more unlikely schemes to date: a collaboration with Roland Petit, the forty-five-year-old avant-garde choreographer who had just established a ballet company in Marseilles. Sporadic discussions about the project had been going on for close to two years, during which Petit's ambitions had been gradually scaled down. Initially, he had aimed at a ballet and movie based on Marcel Proust's *A la Recherche du temps perdu,* variously translated as *Remembrance of Things Past* and *In Search of Lost Time.* An extended autobiographical novel begun in 1913, some of its published versions had stretched to a mind-boggling eighteen volumes; Roger Waters later claimed to have got as far as the second installment of Book I *(Swann's Way),* before coming to a slightly frustrated conclusion—"Fuck this—I can't handle it. It goes too slowly for me."

During early discussions, the group had fleetingly shared very upmarket company indeed: Petit, the iconic Russian dancer Rudolph Nureyev, and the cinematic auteur Roman Polanski, perhaps looking for a suitably upmarket follow-up to his 1971 treatment of *Macbeth.* "That was very funny," says Waters. "It was actually a lunch, with all three of them. We were going to do the music, Petit was going to choreograph it, Nureyev was going to dance it, and Polanski was going to film it. There was a lot of knee-touching under the table and general poovery—and of course, nothing ever came of it: it was a non-starter."

In response to Waters's frustration with Proust, Petit apparently suggested that they attempt a treatment of the anonymously authored—and no less unwieldy—Arabian epic *One Thousand and One Nights,* the sequence of stories that includes such characters as Ali Baba, Sinbad the Sailor, and Aladdin. Waters also recalls the choreographer suggesting a more modern basis for their multimedia bonanza. "I do remember Polanksi saying to Nureyev, 'We could do *Frankenstein*—and Rudy, you could be the fucking monster,'" he says. "But that was the end of that, and they all went to lie in their underpants in the garden.'"

As it turned out, Polanski crashed out of the project, and the Petit company eventually came up with a non-specific ballet based on five Floyd songs: "One of These Days," "Careful with That Axe Eugene," the title track and "When You're In" from *Obscured by Clouds,* and "Echoes." "It started off with very high hopes, and it gradually fizzled and faded down to the Marseilles ballet leaping away to some old bits of music that we cobbled together for the occasion," says Gilmour. "It was a big idea that shrank: a bit of a bodge-up, really." The piece was premiered in Marseilles in November, as the finale of a three-part production that also included two conventional ballet pieces, based on extracts of pieces from Prokofiev,

With Roland Petit and his ballet company in Marseilles, November 1972: "It was a big idea that shrank: a bit of a bodge-up, really." (Nick Mason's Archive)

Shostakovich, Mussorgsky, and Mahler.

Pictures of the event capture the incongruity of the enterprise: the band, hunched over their instruments on a raised stage, while figures in white tights whirl away beneath them. "Because it was all choreographed," says Roger Waters, "although we could ad-lib as much as we wanted to, it had to be the same length every night, or they'd run out of steps. So when we were doing 'Careful with That Axe Eugene,' we had a roadie standing in the wings, with a big set of cards with numbers on them, just counting bars, so we knew that bar 108 was when I screamed, and at bar 256 we had to be finished, because that was the end of their dance."

There were five Marseilles nights, followed in early 1973 by a run of performances in Paris, during which the kind of journalists used to seeing the group play in college halls and smoke-filled theaters turned up to pass judgment on this deeply unlikely venture. Among them was a correspondent from *Sounds,* the British rock weekly aimed at the kind of earnest young men who formed the Floyd's core audience, and hankered after news of their latest creative move forward. That night, however, the appreciation of art seemed to take second place to the performance of one Daniele Jossi, a ballerina partnered by another Petit protégé named Rudy Bryans.

"'Echoes' was the finale," wrote the paper's reporter, "a constantly changing sequence of short pieces, the most spectacular of which were Rudy's entrance from the tunnel, and a dance where he pulled Daniele right across the width of the stage, with her in the splits position."

The Paris ballet performances punctuated the last spate of work at Abbey Road, when the Floyd set about propelling the new record into distinctly futuristic territory. For a few years, they had been in regular touch with Dr. Peter Zinovieff, the founder of a small company called Electronic Music Studios who had played a key role in the BBC Radiophonic Workshop: the electronic sound laboratory that was part of Britain's state broadcasting company. EMS's HQ was at Zinovieff's home in Putney, Southwest London, where he had constructed a twelve-bit computer setup that used an unprecedented 1K of memory—the kind of technology that was usually the preserve of the government and military. "We used to toddle along to his house once in a while," says Gilmour, "and he had a synthesizer that took up the whole of a shed in his garden. It was massive." Photos of Zinovieff's equipment—clearly housed in something both bigger and grander than a "shed"—rather suggest something from the set of *Star Trek.*

By the early 1970s, synthesizers were becoming accessible to rock musicians, thanks also to the equipment pioneered by Robert Moog. The Floyd, whose technophile aspect hardly needs mentioning, were among those

whose heads were turned by the prospects of new, unprecedented sounds—
and by 1972, they had bought two examples of a new compact kind of
machine, both made by Peter Zinovieff's company. The first was a VCS3, a
voltage-controlled synthesizer housed in a kitsch-looking wooden cabinet
that sold for £330 (around $500). It was taken to France for the *Obscured by
Clouds* sessions—though as its droning presence on the title track,
"Childhood's End," and "Absolutely Curtains" proves, the group had initial
difficulties extracting music from it. "To be really honest," says Dave
Gilmour, "we were so thick about it that when we got the first one, we
couldn't make it play different notes. No one had told us how to. You had
to know how to program it to do these things, by twiddling various knobs.
It was an awful lot of effort to get any sound of it at all. On things like
Obscured by Clouds, that's all we were able to do."

By the time of the *Dark Side* session, the VCS3 had been joined by one
of EMS's freshly launched Synthi A machines. A compacted version of the
VCS3—housed in a small suitcase—that cost the band £198 (around $350),
it had the advantage of being compatible with a primitive sequencer, which
opened up a whole new set of possibilities.[6]

According to Alan Parsons, his experience with a Moog synthesizer that
George Harrison owned—whose dimensions were suggestive of a small
telephone exchange—played some role in the band beginning to understand the rudiments of both machines. "I'd had the advantage of working
on the Moog with the Beatles on *Abbey Road,*" he says. "You had to have
a pretty good understanding of voltage control to make it work. It was all
little pin-boards and patch-bays." The Synthi A was later put to work on
"Time" and gave its intro a new boomingly portentous aspect, while the
VCS3 made its way into "Brain Damage." Rick Wright also used the latter
machine, altogether more melodically, for "Any Colour You Like," the
instrumental interlude that linked "Us and Them" and "Brain Damage,"
and recycled the basic chord change that underpinned "Breathe" and
"The Great Gig in the Sky" (this time, it was transposed into a D minor

---

[6] EMS also manufactured a guitar effects unit called the Hi-Fly, used by Dave Gilmour on *The Dark Side of the Moon*.
According to Alan Parsons, "It introduced some of the distortion effects and had good phasing and ADT [Automatic
Double Tracking]." Gilmour is seen using the device in the Abbey Road sequences of *Live at Pompeii*.

"It was all little pin-boards and patch-bays": Waters and the Synthi A, Abbey Road, January 1973. (Taken from the DVD *Live at Pompeii: The Director's Cut*)

7/G progression).

Most noticeably, the Synthi A became the lead instrument on a drastically remodeled version of "The Travel Section." Up until the January sessions, the latter had been a yawn-inducing attempt at something close to jazz-rock fusion, heavy on *Sturm und Drang* but devoid of the evocative power at which the band was aiming. "We'd been playing it live that way for quite some time, as a sort of guitar jam," said Dave Gilmour. "None of us were that happy with it." In the past, Gilmour has also attributed uncertainty about the piece to the additional presence of "Any Colour You Like"; two loose-ended jams were probably one too many.

For whatever reason, "The Travel Section" was redone from scratch as a stripped-down instrumental, based on a run of notes that were programmed into the Synthi A. "I put an eight-note sequence into the Synthi and sped it up," Gilmour later recalled. "Roger thought it wasn't quite right. He put in another, quite like mine, and I hate to say, it was marginally better."

The resulting music was both mesmerizing and frantically fast. Better still, the note sequence was accompanied by a staccato, cymbal-like sound, which lent the piece yet more momentum. "The whole thing—the percussive sound and the bass sequence—was one mono sound, coming out of the Synthi A," says Alan Parsons.

Nonetheless, the piece was given extra momentum by the overdubbing of a Nick Mason hi-hat part. A welter of effects was also grafted onto the track, tying into the band's intention to evoke both a journey and—as Waters puts it—"some kind of crash." A recording of airport announcements was discovered in the Abbey Round record library. Alan Parsons recorded the footsteps of Peter James, his assistant engineer, walking across the studio floor. Gilmour drew ghostly guitar noises from a guitar by playing it using a mic stand, which were then run backwards. On top of all that, the Synthi A was also used for atonal bursts of sound that panned between left and right, thus evoking movement—"a Doppler effect," as

Dave Gilmour puts it. Finally, there was the hellish explosion that ended the piece, once again lifted from the Abbey Road library.

While such work was proceeding, the band also had guests: the French film director Adrian Maben and a small film crew, equipped with one 35mm camera, there to shoot new footage for a recut version of *Live at Pompeii*.[7] The idea of grafting additional elements onto the movie had been hatched by Maben and Roger Waters while the pair were on a brief fishing trip; with Waters's blessing, Maben was keen to film the band in the studio so as to augment his concert movie with a sense of Pink Floyd actually bringing their music into being.

Rick Wright, "the great unsung hero of the Floyd," delivering the piano part of "Us and Them" (Taken from the DVD *Live at Pompeii: The Director's Cut*)

He succeeded in his aim, though the footage of the group at work—Waters dubbing Synthi A parts onto the intro of "Time" and demonstrating the construction of "On the Run," Gilmour adding a lead guitar part to "Brain Damage" that was later discarded, a wonderfully understated sequence in which Rick Wright records a piano track for "Us and Them"—is far less compelling than sequences in which Maben talks to the band and films them in the Abbey Road canteen (where they attest to their middle-class Englishness by taking "supper"). Here, one quickly gets a sense of each member's defining traits, and the way the group's personalities lock into the larger whole.

Roger Waters is the dominant presence, answering Maben's questions with a sense of slightly petulant impatience, and stridently contributing to the dinner-time conversation. "We all know that you're God almighty, Roger," says a disembodied voice, just before Waters attempts to skewer another associate's claim that a detailed knowledge of music need not be a

7 The first version of *Live at Pompeii* was premiered at the Edinburgh Film Festival in September 1972. The next version, featuring footage shot at Abbey Road, went on general release in 1974, and was subsequently released on video. In 2003, a DVD subtitled *The Director's Cut* appeared, including additional black-and-white sequences shot in Paris in December 1972.

prerequisite for a successful career as a record producer, with reference to Pink Floyd's manager. "A record producer," says Waters, adopting the withering tones of an exasperated schoolteacher, "is someone who's in charge of a recording session. *Right?* And in order to be in charge of a recording session, you need to have … a fairly extensive knowledge of what the equipment's about, and what music's about, and what rock 'n' roll's about…. Steve [O'Rourke] knows what rock 'n' roll's about, [but] he's got *no idea* what the equipment's about, and he's got very little idea—in terms of technicalities—what the music's about. He knows what he likes."

"Plenty of people have produced records on that basis," says another voice. "Very successful records."

"Who?" asks Waters, before appearing to correct himself. "Whom? *Whom?*" His grammar is actually mistaken, though it only underlines his own kind of alpha-male super-confidence.

Gilmour, meanwhile, is noticeably less confrontational. His brand of self-assurance is manifested in a wry air of detachment, embodied by his answer to a question about the seemingly unbreakable link between Pink Floyd and what remains of the drug culture. "It's an image we'd like to dispel," he says. "I think it was very heavy a few years ago…. It's not so bad since, but I still think that most people see us as a very drug-orientated group." He pauses. "Of course, we're not," he adds. His face then breaks into the merest of smiles. "You can trust us."

Rick Wright, tellingly, is not interviewed. The eternally emollient Nick Mason, however, good-humoredly parries Maben's inquiries, and dispenses answers laced with an appealing kind of irony, and the occasional penetrating insight. "We share the same sense of humor to some extent," he tells Maben. "We lust after money to some extent. And we have a lot of interest

Waters plays the bass part of "Brain Damage/Eclipse." "That song is saying, 'There you are, that's all there is to it: What you experience is what life is.'" (Taken from the DVD *Live at Pompeii: The Director's Cut*)

in what we're doing together." In the context of Pink Floyd's later history, his next thought is prescient indeed. "I think that's really when the thing breaks down—when one person finds that what he's doing doesn't interest him, or he feels he could do something better by himself."

Hindsight casts early 1973 as an auspicious time for Pink Floyd: they were, after all, on the verge of completing the album that would cut through their last associations with the long-gone days of psychedelia and secure their reputation as a very modern kind of rock group. Mason, however, evidently worried about whether they could make such a leap. "Unfortunately, we mark a sort of era," he says, a little later in the film. "We're in danger of becoming a relic of the past. For some people, we represent their childhood: 1967, underground London, the free concert in Hyde Park and so on." Though the success of *Dark Side* would finally exorcise such ghosts, at least one member of Pink Floyd could still sense their chilly presence.

5

BALANCED ON THE BIGGEST WAVE:
DARK SIDE, PHASE THREE

"I thought it was a terrific idea," says Roger Waters. "I wrote all the questions down on a set of cards, and they were in sequence. A *ton* of people did it. Each person would read the top card and answer it—with no one else in the room—and then take that card off, and do the next one. So, for instance, when it said, 'When was the last time you were violent?', they would answer that, and the next card said, 'Were you in the right?' The idea was to stimulate people to speak in ways that would provide essential color for the record."

It was toward the end of the *Dark Side* sessions that Waters came up with one of his most inspired schemes: accentuating the themes that underlay his grand concept by streaking the music with human voices, answering questions that tapped into the concerns expressed in his lyrics. Waters recalls around fifteen questions in total: by way of warming up the interviewees, they began with such innocuous inquiries as "What's your favorite color?" and "What's your favorite food?" before edging into more powerful areas. Waters's inquiries about violence were thus joined by questions relating to insanity ("Do you ever think you're going mad?"), death ("Are you afraid of dying?"), and one last inquiry about the album itself: "What's *The Dark Side of the Moon* all about?"

The cast the band required came from two sources: the staff and temporary occupants of Abbey Road ("I'd hook people in from the corridor—whoever was in the building," says Waters), and Pink Floyd's road crew, some of whom were at Abbey Road to assist the band: their road manager Peter Watts and his girlfriend (known, for some reason, as Puddie), a gruff-voiced northern Englishman named Chris Adamson, a character known to all as Liverpool Bobby, and a semi-legendary roadie called Roger "The Hat" Manifold, whose amusingly skewed take on life suggested that he would be an ideal subject.

By the time the latter was tracked down, Waters had mislaid his cards, so his interview was conducted as a standard dialogue. Possibly assisted by a joint or two, the conversation started with Manifold jovially setting down his terms—"If I participate in this fucking effort, I hope I'm going to get my gold disc at the end of it"—before the interview process began in earnest. The highlights of the tape, broadcast in an English radio documentary in 1976, run as follows:

RW: You see … what would be best really … I mean I might have to prompt you occasionally. I might even have to ask you a question … but what would be best would be if you could just tell us about it …'cos I've told you what the record's about.

RM: Right—but tell you about it in what way?

RW: Any way you like.

RM: Ooohhh …

RW: You want me to ask you some questions?

RM: I think that would be better, man.

RW: 'Cos you've been on the road for ten years, right, so it's all happened—so we want to know just what you think about various things …

RM: Dig it. *Dig it!*

RW: Like life in bands, and life on the road, and what you think of other things as well.

RM: Right.

RW: Now, something that's very interesting, for instance, is, What's your personal opinion … why do you think a lot of bands split up?

RM: Egotism, I would say. Er … I would say mainly egotism. That's one reason. There's many others, man, but that's one. I would say that's … um … the one that immediately comes to mind. Egotism.

RW: I think I'd go along with that.

RM: Mmmmm. I mean—you should know what musicians are like.

RW: What are musicians like?

RM: Well, you see, really they should be normal people … but someone once said to me that a proper artist has got a right to be temperamental. I think I've been unfortunate in meeting every temperamental artist in the business. Nah! They're temperamental, that's all.

RW: Why do you think they're temperamental?

RM: Because of the nature of the work they're doing.

RW: Do you think it might be because they get too much power?

RM: No—definitely not. I would say too much stress on themselves. [They're] given false ideals.… How's it going?

RW: Alright.

RM: *Far out.*

RW: I'll take a bit of that for me, you don't mind if I give you some do you?

RM: Help yourself.

RW: Right …

RM: The initial shock's over!

RW: OK. That was a very good answer.

RM: Thank you. Do I get ten out of ten for that?

RW: Yeah.

RM: Far out.

RW: You get eleven out of ten for that one. [Lights what may or may not be a cigarette, coughs] Right, what else was there? I'll tell you what another bit of it was about, which [Liverpool] Bobby could probably have got into but I don't think it was explained enough in the question, so he didn't really get into talking about it—and that is … there's a track on the record about violence, right …

RM: Oh yeah. I'm into that.

RW: And it's called "Us and Them," simply because when you're in a violent situation there's always like *you,* who's …

RM: Dig it.

RW: Right … and there's *them.* And they're two very different things. And one of the questions we asked the others was, When was the last time you thumped somebody?, Why did you do it?, Do you think you were in the right?

RM: Oh yeah. The last time that I thumped someone was only the other day, as a matter of fact. I was driving along the road towards Northwood Hills where my brother lives, and this cat in front of me was driving his car and all of a sudden he stopped and opened his door, and from where I was in my truck, I could see that he never looked in his mirror—he just opened his door, which caused me to swerve on the other side of the road, very narrowly missing an oncoming motor car. So I pulled in, and like a gentleman I went up to him and said, "Now look man—like, *that ain't cool.* Right, the thing to do man, if you're gonna stop your car, you stop, you look in your mirror, and if there's nothing about you open your door. But you never done that, and like, it nearly cost me my life." Well, the guy was very rude … In fact, his last words to me were, he called me a "long-haired git." So, I felt compelled. Well, seeing as he was that rude, I had to … retribution was close at hand. So that was the last time I was violent, about three days ago.

RW: Do you think you were justified? You put one on him …

RM: Definitely, yeah, definitely. 'Cos the thing is, man, when you're driving on the road, I mean like, you get a person who's that rude—I mean, they're gonna kill you. So like, if you give them a quick, short, sharp shock, they don't do it again. Dig it? I mean, he got off lightly 'cos I could've given him a thrashing—I only hit him once! [Laughs]

RW: Right. Now another thing that we're interested in … there's a track on the album that's supposed to be about it … pegging out.

RM: Cor … evil bastard!

RW: How do you feel about that? Are you frightened of it?

RM: Death? *Wow.* What is it man—you tell me. I don't know. I once had my head read by … this chick that was into astrology. I gave her my date of birth and everything—can you dig that? And she, like, told me where all my energy was channeled, and she said one of them was "experiences." So, like, when I come across death it'll be a new trip won't it? So, like, I wouldn't have had it before, so it'll be all right. [Laughs] Doesn't bother me in the slightest. Live for today, gone tomorrow. That's me. Yeah—don't worry about it. Never have done. Something new, isn't it?

RW: Do you think you ever will … I mean, when you're a bit closer to it?

RM: Nah, nah—well, it's one of them things that never goes out of fashion, isn't it? [Laughs]

Aside from Pink Floyd's crew, Waters's questions were also answered by a clutch of people from outside the band's circle. Gerry O'Driscoll, a middle-aged Irishman who was one of Abbey Road's janitorial "browncoats," contributed a set of plain-spoken answers that peaked with his reply to the question about the album's title: "There is no dark side in the moon, really. As a matter of fact, it's all dark. The only thing that makes it look light is the sun."

In addition, a few slightly more famous names agreed to participate. Paul McCartney's 1970s enterprise Wings were also in Abbey Road, working on the album that would be called *Red Rose Speedway*. Waters thus

(top) Roger "The Hat" Manifold, the roadie whose opinions crystallized some of the album's key themes: "If you give them a quick, short, sharp shock, they don't do it again…."

(bottom) Gerry O'Driscoll, the Abbey Road "browncoat" cajoled into a *Dark Side* interview: "There is no dark side in the moon, really. As a matter of fact, it's all dark…." (Courtesy of Alan Brown)

grabbed the the band's Irish guitarist Henry McCullough—who answered the violence questions with the memory of an incident from New Year's Eve 1972, when he had been "too drunk" to remember if he was in the right—and Paul McCartney. In the recollection of David Gilmour, the ex-Beatle was too evasive to provide any satisfactory material. "He was too clever; too guarded," he says. "He didn't want to give anything away. We needed people that were open and direct."

Roger Waters, however, claims that McCartney's unsuitability was based on another problem entirely. "He was the only person who found it necessary to *perform,* which was useless, of course. I thought it was really interesting, that he would do that. He was trying to be *funny,* which wasn't what we wanted at all."

McCartney was not the only interviewee whose contributions fell to the cutting-room floor. Alan Parsons also agreed to participate, awkwardly sitting through Waters's questions, before reaching the final card, and being forced to consider what the music he had spent much of the last seven months poring over actually meant. "I made a bit of a fool of myself," he says. The question was, "What do you think *Dark Side of the Moon* is all about?" "And I really had no idea at all. I didn't give a sufficiently interesting answer to have it used on the album."

The material that was combined with the music, however, worked a brilliant kind of magic. The underlying theme of insanity was perfectly crystallized by the manic laughter of Peter Watts, the words of Chris Adamson—"I've been mad for fucking years—absolutely years"—and a wonderfully emphatic contribution from Gerry O'Driscoll: "I've always been mad. I know I've been mad like most of us have. Very hard to explain why you were mad, even if you're not mad." The latter excels himself once again on "The Great Gig in the Sky": "I am not frightened of dying. Any time will do; I don't mind. Why should I be frightened of dying? There's no reason for it—you've got to go sometime."

"Us and Them"'s lament for the fact that human conflict is so

(opposite) Waters with Floyd roadies Alan Styles (far left) and Peter Watts, whose manic laughter was a perfect addition to the album. (Nick Mason's Archive)

commonplace as to seem utterly mundane gets reflected back onto the music by a collage of quotations from the aforementioned Puddie, Henry McCullough, O'Driscoll, and Chris Adamson, brought into play in the midst of the fade-out of "Money." Six minutes later comes the voice of Roger Manifold: "I mean, they're gonna kill you. So like, if you give them a quick, short, sharp shock, they don't do it again. Dig it? I mean, he got off lightly 'cos I could've given him a thrashing—I only hit him once…. Good manners don't cost nothing, do they?"

Perhaps the key reason such moments were so successful lay in their reflection of Roger Waters's most important intention. In writing about the fundamental aspects of modern living, and articulating them with a deliberate lack of artifice and affectation, he was clearly aiming at summing up truly universal experiences—in which sense, the chorus of thoughts, anecdotes, and contentions that peppered the record made perfect sense, implicitly extending its reach way beyond the life of four English musicians, and into the realm of the everyman. In Waters's own estimation, the voices were "human and truthful … they had a poignancy and power that was all their own."

By the time the spoken elements were added to the music, Pink Floyd and Alan Parsons had been joined by a new creative accomplice. Chris Thomas was a twenty-six-year-old producer who had entered the profession via the esteemed George Martin, with whom he had worked on *The Beatles,* better known as The White Album; aside from his work in the control room, he played mellotron on "The Continuing Story of Bungalow Bill," and harpischord on George Harrison's "Piggies." From there, he had gone on to develop his talent through work with Procol Harum, before producing *Paris 1919,* the critically admired album that marked a watershed for the founding Velvet Underground member John Cale—and was put to tape just before Thomas's arrival at Abbey Road.

Alan Parsons, whose opinions on Thomas's contribution are still char-

acterized by the merest hint of resentment, later described the thinking behind his arrival as follows: "The band felt they needed a fresh pair of ears … which was probably a justified thought." Roger Waters later claimed that Thomas's appointment allayed the problem of simple exhaustion; the band, he said, had "run out of energy." David Gilmour, by contrast, has long believed that Thomas was brought in as a means of finding a way through a key divide between him and Waters, partly based on the latter's fondness for the stripped-back ambience he had so admired on *John Lennon/Plastic Ono Band*. "Roger and I were, as usual, arguing and bickering about how things should be in the overall mix," said Gilmour, some thirty years later. "I favored a wetter, more echoey sound, and things like the voices appearing more subtly within the mush of the mix. Roger wanted things to be drier and cleaner and clearer."

His memories chime with those of Nick Mason: "Dave wanted a bit more echo on, and Roger liked things drier. And one of the reasons Dave was particularly pleased with the idea of using Chris Thomas to mix the album was that he knew that Chris liked that more echoey sound, so he thought things would go more his way."

Thomas, only furthering the confusion, later claimed that such accounts had precious little foundation in reality. "There was no difference of opinion between them," he said. "I don't remember Roger once saying that he wanted less echo. In fact, there were never any hints they were later going to fall out. It was a very creative atmosphere. A lot of fun."

Whatever the thinking behind Thomas's appointment, Nick Mason attests to what actually mattered: the input of this newcomer to the sessions ensured that both parties were eventually content. "What's great is, I've never heard either Dave or Roger say, 'Well, the trouble is, it would have been better if there had just been a bit more—or less—echo,'" Mason says. "Chris got it right."

The band may have quickly appreciated his input—but at first, Thomas was at least mildly disappointed by what he heard. *The Dark Side of the Moon,* he later claimed, seemed to be an admirable collection of individual pieces, but he had expected something more along the lines of the drawn-out, florid experiments on which they had built so much of their post–Syd Barrett work. "The album before that was *Meddle,* which had 'Echoes' on it, and I had hoped they were going to get into something like that," he later reflected. "But *Dark Side* was just a bunch of songs. Bunches of songs are what I always did, so I thought, 'Great—Pink Floyd. I'll get to do something out of the ordinary.' But that wasn't really the case."

Having allowed this feeling of anticlimax to wane, Thomas began work. The album's sleeve would accord him an understated "Mix Supervised by" credit, though he has always claimed that his role was a little wider. "I was brought in at the end of the record, but as a producer," he later said. "It wasn't just mixing—it was mixing and recording."

Thomas's period in the studio certainly saw large changes to the music the band had put to tape. For example, the material's innate sense of space was further developed by inspired instances of the songs being pared down.

Early takes of "Brain Damage" and "Us and Them" saw them slightly cluttered by Dave Gilmour's squalling lead guitar and Dick Parry's sax respectively; now, as such embellishments were reduced, the songs took on a new immediacy. Better still, the vocal on the latter song was treated with a beat-perfect echo ("Us … us …us … us … us/And them … them … them") which served to underline the universal reach of its sentiments; in the later concerts that followed the album's release, an accompanying film showing huge crowds of London commuters would make the point explicit.

At Thomas's suggestion, "Money" was bolstered by the addition of more guitar: "I thought it was such a great riff that I got them to track the guitars to build it up." He also worked on the last-minute creation of "Speak to Me," the minute-long overture modeled on the taped introduction to *Dark Side* that had been in place from the start, and named after Alan Parsons's opening instructions to Waters's spoken-word interviewees. Sprinkled with elements from the songs already put to tape (the clocks from "Time," the tape loop from "Money"), it also drew on three other sounds: the simulated heartbeat, looped from a recording of Nick Mason's bass drum, that would also bring the album to a close; snatches of speech and laughter from Gerry O'Driscoll, Chris Adamson, and Peter Watts; and a helicopter effect—shades of Vietnam, perhaps?—extracted from the Synthi A. The piece was credited to Nick Mason, who has claimed credit for "an assembly that I did with the existing music." Roger Waters went on to assert his authorship, tracing his colleague's credit to a fit of generosity.

Perhaps most notably, it was while Chris Thomas was at Abbey Road that the band recorded one of *Dark Side*'s most transcendent elements. "The Great Gig in the Sky" was still unfinished: combined, during its live

David Gilmour, pictured while attempting abortive final overdubs on "Brain Damage." "After an amazing guitar solo, Roger would say something like, 'Oh, I think we might be able to get away with that one, Dave.'" (Taken from the DVD *Live at Pompeii: The Director's Cut*)

renditions, with the Christian voices that dated back to its first incarnation as an organ piece, but in need of something that little bit more arresting. It remains unclear who suggested a female singer might take it to completion ("I've no idea whose idea it was to have someone wailing on it," says Waters), but the idea of bringing in a session vocalist named Clare Torry—whose vocals would also define the climactic moment of "Speak to Me"—was definitely down to Alan Parsons.

"She had done a covers album," he says. "I can remember that she did 'Light My Fire,' and I can't for the life of me remember anything else about it. It was a popular thing at the time to do cover versions and put them out on compilations: this was before anyone realized you could get the original tracks. I just thought Clare had a great voice. When the situation came up, the band started head-scratching, saying, 'Who are we going to get to sing over this?' I said, 'I've got an idea—I know this girl; I think she'd be really good for it.'"

Torry, then twenty-two, split her time between work as a session singer and her duties as a staff songwriter with a U.K. publisher called Valley Music. She had indeed appeared on an array of covers-based compilation albums—alongside such session singers as the still-unknown Elton John—but she has no memory of the song mentioned by Parsons. "I don't remember *ever* singing 'Light My Fire,'" she says. "And if it was on a compilation covers album, the boys always did boys' vocals. They were soundalike records. One thing I've never been accused of is sounding like Jim Morrison." In her recollection, she had actually made Parsons's acquaintance while contributing to an earlier session at Abbey Road.

Whatever, Torry was initially called in mid-January, and asked if she could come to the studio at very short notice. "I didn't know much about Pink Floyd," she says. "I knew 'See Emily Play,' but even that hadn't really hit the spot with me. They weren't my favorite band. If it had been the Kinks, I'd have been over the moon." Her other commitments—in tandem, perhaps, with her indifference to the Floyd—meant that the band had to

Clare Torry. Her contribution to "The Great Gig in the Sky" was *Dark Side*'s final masterstroke. "I thought, 'Maybe I should just pretend I'm an instrument....'" (Courtesy of Clare Torry)

wait at least a week: having negotiated a fee of £30 (around $50), Torry arrived at Abbey Road on the evening of Sunday, January 21.

"They didn't say very much," she recalls. "Dave Gilmour was the only one who really communicated with me. That's my abiding memory. I went in and they just said, 'Well, we're making this album, and there's this track—and we don't really know what to do.' They told me what the album was about: birth, and death, and everything in between. I thought it was rather pretentious, to be honest. And I said, 'Well, play me the track.' They did that, and I said, 'What do you want?' They said, 'We don't *know.*'"

In Torry's recollection, the piece's underlying theme of death did not really enter into the conversation; Gilmour's very general instruction was to ensure that her contribution was somehow "emotional." "I said, 'Let me go out into the studio, put some headphones on, and have a go,'" she says. "I started going 'Ooh-aah, baby, baby—yeah, yeah.' They said, 'No no—if we wanted that we'd have got Doris Troy.' They said, 'Try some longer notes.' And as this went on, I was getting more familiar with the backing track. There was a bit more conversation, and I remember thinking to myself, 'I really, really do not know what to do. And perhaps it would be better if I said, 'Thank you very much' and gave up. It wasn't getting anywhere: it was just *nothing.*

"That was when I thought, 'Maybe I should just pretend I'm an instrument.' So I said, 'Start the track again.' One of my most enduring memories is that there was a lovely can [i.e. headphone] balance. Alan Parsons got a lovely sound on my voice: echoey, but not too echoey. It was just all-enveloping, which for a singer, is always inspirational.

"I started getting this pattern of notes," she says, "and they said, 'Well, that seems the right direction to go.' And I told them to put the tape on. At the end of the first take, Dave Gilmour said, 'Do another one—but even *more* emotional.' So I did a second take. And he said, 'I think we could do a better one.' I started, and halfway through I realized that I was beginning to be repetitive; derivative. It was beginning to sound contrived. I said, 'I think you've got enough.' I actually thought it sounded like caterwauling.

"I think Rick Wright has subsequently said I was embarrassed," she says. "And I *was.* I said, 'Thank you very much,' and off I went. By ten o'clock, I was having dinner with my boyfriend." If Torry's account suggests a businesslike kind of efficiency, she also recalls—not entirely surprisingly—that her performance in the studio was more than a little draining. "It was *extremely* tiring," she says. "I had beads of sweat on me. I couldn't do it now: I'd have to have a half-hour interval."

Though the band's response to what she had recorded seems to have been couched in their customary understatement, they were quietly thrilled. "She didn't really look the part," says Dave Gilmour. "We had to encourage her a little bit. We gave her some dynamic hints: 'Perhaps you'd like to do this piece quietly, and this piece louder.' But she was fantastic."

His praise is hardly misplaced. Torry's contribution gloriously succeeded where spoken-word tape effects and Parsons's NASA recordings had so far failed, tapping into the tumultuous drama to which the group aspired—not least when she dispensed wails that could variously be interpreted as either orgasmic or terrifying (or both). With a matter of weeks until *Dark Side* made the cut, she had delivered its last missing triumph.

As she walked away from Abbey Road, however, Torry assumed that what had been put to tape would probably be rejected. "It seemed a bit screechy-screechy," she says. "I really thought it would never see the light of day."

Since 1968, Pink Floyd's recording sessions had formed the backdrop to a recurrent ritual: visits to the studio by Storm Thorgeson and Aubrey Powell (also known as Po), there to receive word of what wonders were planned for the band's new album and thereby begin work on the accompanying sleeve art. The information they received would be fed into a web of ideas that was constantly being augmented and updated; in Powell's recollection, the Floyd's old Cambridge associates were as creatively hyperactive as the band. "I tended to be the one who did the business and the photography. Storm, without any question, was the dominant design partner. He had a great take on image and design; I worked on the execution of the idea—the style to his content.

"The way Hipgnosis worked was this: usually, we would work all day in the studio, and then twice a week, we'd meet at about nine o'clock at night, and work till three in the morning, having an ideas think-tank: maybe just Storm and myself, or some other friends would join us, or the guy who did our printing might be there. We'd sit down and chew the fat for a bit: 'There's a Pink Floyd album coming out. We've got some lyrics here. What do you think?'

"Nick Mason and Roger were the ones who were the most tuned in to what we were doing," he continues. "They were always at the forefront. Nick always had humorous asides to say about things, and Roger was very forthright about what he felt would work. But they never changed any of the designs we did. There was never anything like, 'Couldn't you put a suburban house in the field behind the cow?' They were very good at leaving us to deliver."

Though the band tended to happily allow Thorgeson and Powell something close to artistic autonomy, the designs they worked up for the Floyd could usually be guaranteed to incur the ire of the rather more straight-laced minds at the band's record company. By the early 1970s, the idea that album covers might also stand as examples of fine art was rapidly gaining ground, but plenty of EMI's London staff expected designs that would simply assist in the selling of the record within. The solitary cow on the front of *Atom Heart Mother,* therefore, caused no end of disquiet. "The record company were apoplectic," says Powell. "It was, 'What the *fuck* is this thing?' They had no concept of something that was so original and different.

"There was this guy called Ron Dunton: this big, jolly fat man who

(opposite) Waters and Gilmour share their thoughts with Storm Thorgeson, the "dominant design partner" of Hipgnosis. For him, *Dark Side* was bound up with "the theme of madness—the madness of rock 'n' roll and madness in general." (Jill Furmanovsky)

(this page) Aubrey "Po" Powell, backstage in Birmingham, England, with Waters and Gilmour. "When *The Dark Side of the Moon* was mentioned, it was alway clearly in the context of the back of the mind; some-thing to do with the unknown." (Jill Furmanovsky) was in charge of the album cover department. And whenever you went in there with something, he'd say, 'Well, what do you call that then? What's that?' He *hated* Storm and me. 'Where's the lettering? What do you mean, there isn't going to be any? Well, I'd better speak to somebody upstairs about that.' But because we were employed by the band, we had power. It felt great to stand our ground and say, 'Well, that's what it is.'"

If hindsight casts Ron Dunton as the hopelessly square opponent of designs that would eventually become iconic, it should be borne in mind that even by their own admission, some of Hipgnosis's work could get a little too abstract. The period immediately before *The Dark Side of the Moon* threw up two perfect examples: the sleeve art for *Obscured by Clouds,* an indecipherably out-of-focus photograph of a male character from Barbet Schroeder's movie; and the image that adorned *Meddle*—a human ear overlaid with a picture of droplets of water. "Water is variable yet controllable," Thorgeson retrospectively explained. "Water lights beautifully. Water is evocative, serene, haunting, powerful."

Powell, however, has a rather more damning opinion. "*Meddle* was a mess. I hated that cover. I don't think we did them justice with that at all; it's half-hearted." At the time, he had the sense that his misgivings were also shared by the band: "I think it was the kind of thing they wanted to get away from. And I think also, there'd probably been a word in their ear from the record company and their management."

By early 1973, therefore, just as it was imperative for Pink Floyd to finally escape the shadows of the Syd Barrett era, so Thorgeson and Powell could feel the distinct sense that it was time for their own definitive move forward. "The Floyd were either going to be a mediocre band, carrying on doing the kind of things they'd done in the past ... because you've got to remember, the hippie thing was starting to fade out by now," says Powell. "They had to *go* somewhere or slip away. It was crucial that something would come out of the album. The same thing applied to the design."

What was required was quickly crystallized in an instruction from an unlikely source indeed: Rick Wright, who told Powell and Thorgeson that they should aim at something "smarter, neater—more classy."

Powell and Thorgeson duly set about divining the kind of themes that might color their designs. "I'd had various conversations with the band about what they wanted on the sleeve," Thorgeson later recalled. "Roger explained the intellectual thrust of the music; the theme of madness—the madness of rock 'n' roll and madness in general."

"When *The Dark Side of the Moon* was mentioned," says Aubrey Powell, "it was always clearly in the context of the back of the mind; something to do with the unknown. Because at the time, the dark side of the moon *was* unknown. It was always considered to be a metaphor for the other side of madness. For me, that was always clearly understood."

What Thorgeson and Powell came up with, however, had a rather fuzzy—if not pretty much nonexistent—link to such concerns. The image of a prism had been in their minds for a while, thanks—in Powell's recollection, at least—to a book that Thorgeson had brought to one of their "think-tank" sessions. "In the meetings we used to have, Storm always had loads of books around. We often used to crib pictures for initial ideas. And one of the books we had, which had been done in the '40s or '50s, was full of black and white photographs, with one or two color ones. One of the pictures that was in it was of a glass prism, lying on a piece of sheet music, with a light being shone through it. And on the other side of it, across the sheet music, was the spectrum. I can remember Storm saying, 'Isn't that a great image?'" A suitably prismatic Hipgnosis design was soon proposed as the motif for a new British record label called Clearlight, but nothing came of the idea.

When the idea was revived and applied to Pink Floyd's new album, Thorgeson claimed to see all kinds of connections. "It represented both the diversity and cleanliness of the sound of the music," he said. "In a more conscious way, it worked for a band with a reputation for their light show."

There were also more conceptual ideas at work: "The triangle is a symbol for ambition, one of the themes that Roger was concerned with … you had several ideas coming together at once."

In addition to its relevance to the group, Aubrey Powell sensed a vague connection to their audience. "Rainbow colors were very much the colors of choice of the hippie nation," he says. "The band weren't hippies by this time, but it was definitely symbolic of the kind of people who were buying Pink Floyd records. And I think the idea of a singular point refracting into these beautiful colors was also symbolic: from this one group came all these multifarious colors."

Despite the strengths of the prism image—worked up as a rough design using black cardboard and strips of colored paper—Thorgeson and Powell eventually offered the group a range of ideas, stretching to somewhere in the region of ten designs. Most have been lost to history: "The only thing I remember is that none of them involved the moon," says Powell. "I think we talked about cheese for a while, but that didn't get past the drawing board." Thirty-three years on, he can only recall one alternative idea: a sleeve built around the Marvel Comics character the Silver Surfer, rather echoing the presence of Dr. Strange on *A Saucerful of Secrets*. "We were all into Marvel Comics, and the Silver Surfer seemed to be another fantastic singular image. We never would have got permission to use it. But we liked the image of a silver man, on a silver surfboard, scooting across the universe. It had mystical, mythical properties." He laughs. "Very *cosmic,* man."

The various options were eventually presented to the band. "It was at Abbey Road," says Powell. "It was all quite moody, as I remember. The lights were down. And Storm and I laid the artworks, twelve by twelve sketches, around their instruments. And Roger looked at the rough of the prism design and said, 'That's it.' Nick immediately went the same way, followed by Dave and Rick."

"I don't know quite why it made sense," says Gilmour. "When Storm showed us all the ideas, with that one, there was no doubt: That is *it*. It's a brilliant cover. One can look at it after that first moment of brilliance and think, 'Well, it's a very commercial idea: it's very stark and simple; it'll look great in shop windows.' It wasn't a nice picture of four lads bouncing around in the countryside. That fact wasn't lost on us."

There was no original artwork for *The Dark Side of the Moon*. The prism design—in its execution, the work of a Hipgnosis employee called George Hardie—was sketched out in a set of instructions to EMI's printers, who rendered the sleeve as a "mechanical tint lay." "It wasn't difficult to create at all," says Aubrey Powell. "And I was actually against it, because being the kind of photographic type, I wanted to photograph the prism and do it for real. It seemed a bit cold; dispiriting, almost. But I got shouted down."

As the idea progressed, the usually fusty minds at EMI informed the band that more money might be available. Roger Waters was thus able to subtly amend the Hipgnosis plan, allowing for the inclusion of an element that would reflect the album's opening and closing sound. "At first," says Waters, "it was just a square—and then the record company told us they'd pay for a gatefold, so I said, 'Why don't we run the colors through the middle and stick the image of a heartbeat across it?' And that was it."

At Thorgeson's suggestion, another prism picture was added to the back cover, allowing a circular image, whereby light entered one prism, was split into the spectrum, eventually hit another, became a single beam again … and so on. As Thorgeson quickly realized, the idea would also allow record stores to create continuous displays, simply by placing the front cover, inner gatefold, and back cover next to each other. "What a fabulous shop window display, stretching right across the window, right round the shop interior, out the door and into the street," he wrote in his 1997 memoir-cum-portfolio *Mind over Matter*. "All this concentrated commercial thinking got us nowhere. I never did see this attribute being utilized in the sale and promotion of *The Dark Side of the Moon*."

By way of salesmanship, however, Hipgnosis came up with another scheme. *The Dark Side of the Moon* would come with small stickers, featuring stylized, cartoon-like images of the Egyptian pyramids and a red moon—and two posters. One would be based on an array of photographs of the band playing live; the other would feature an image of the Egyptian monuments, captured on infrared film. The latter idea, much to Thorgeson and Powell's delight, entailed a trip abroad: rather than sourcing suitable images from a photographic library, they were craftily set on taking their own pictures.

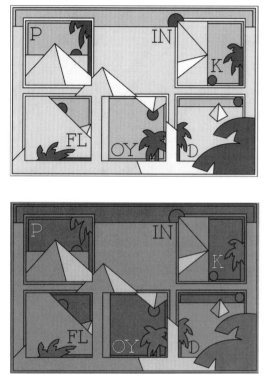

The Dark Side of the Moon would come with small stickers.

So it was that Aubrey Powell accompanied Thorgeson, his girlfriend Libby, and their son Bill on a trip to Egypt. "It was quite eerie," he says. "In those days, there wasn't a big tourist industry in Egypt at all. It was a question of renting a battered old car, and driving out to the pyramids, and sorting out one or two strange people with camels with a bit of money.... I always remember going out there at night. It was bitterly cold, and there was a moon up. It was *really* spooky. There was absolutely no one around.

"On the first two days and nights, Storm and I went out there, and we shot hundreds of photographs, from every angle: close up, in the distance, different lighting, infrared, black and white, color. And after the second day, I suddenly went down with the worst runs you could think of. The Nile was coming out of my bum. So I had to stay behind that night, and Storm went out there and shot the infrared pictures that were used on the posters."

Powell's complaint also struck Thorgeson's girlfriend and son, meaning that Thorgeson saw out the rest of the assignment alone. "I ended up on my own in the middle of the night, standing before the awesome pyramids beneath a full moon, not a soul around and scared shitless," he wrote in *Mind over Matter*. "Then in the dead of night, three figures approached …

three arab soldiers with guns. All my stereotyped xenophobic fears swept rapidly across my mind. I could see the headlines: 'Slit from ear to ear, young photographer found in desert, buggered to death, beaten and tortured'. . . . The soldiers were, of course, quite friendly, and informed me that I was on Egyptian army land, and should consider going home forthwith. But I needed to continue taking photographs . . . a little money seemed to do the trick, and they left, muttering something about crazy English people."

Back in the safer confines of Abbey Road, work on *The Dark Side of the Moon* drew to a close on February 19, 1973. By modern standards, it was the conclusion of a taxing process whereby the various elements of the music had to be manually manipulated, while the transitions between the piece's individual songs were nipped, tucked, and cross-faded. Not for nothing did Dave Gilmour later comment that "a mix in those days was a performance, every bit as much as doing a gig." On top of all that, given that Pink Floyd were operating in the age of vinyl, *Dark Side* had to be bisected into sides One and Two: the crucial division came at the close of "The Great Gig in the Sky," leaving the tape loop from "Money" to open the record's second installment.

In keeping with the reasons for his arrival at the sessions, responsibility for the final mix lay chiefly with Chris Thomas—who, in Gilmour's recollection, fulfilled his brief by successfully plotting a way through the tensions running between him and Roger Waters ("He helped to find a compromise between the way I saw it and the way Roger saw it"). To some extent, a midpoint between Gilmour's alleged fondness for a "wet," echo-laden sound and Waters's drier tastes defined the sound of the finished record: the aural dimensions of *Dark Side* were boosted by Thomas's masterly use of reverb, but the musical economy on display—embodied in the band's innate sense of understatement, and Thomas's paring back of such tracks as "Us and Them" and "Brain Damage"—reined it back from any kind of grandiosity. *The Dark Side of the Moon* was thus both impressive

155

Storm Thorgeson: "It was bitterly cold, and there was a moon up. It was *really* spooky. There was absolutely no one around."

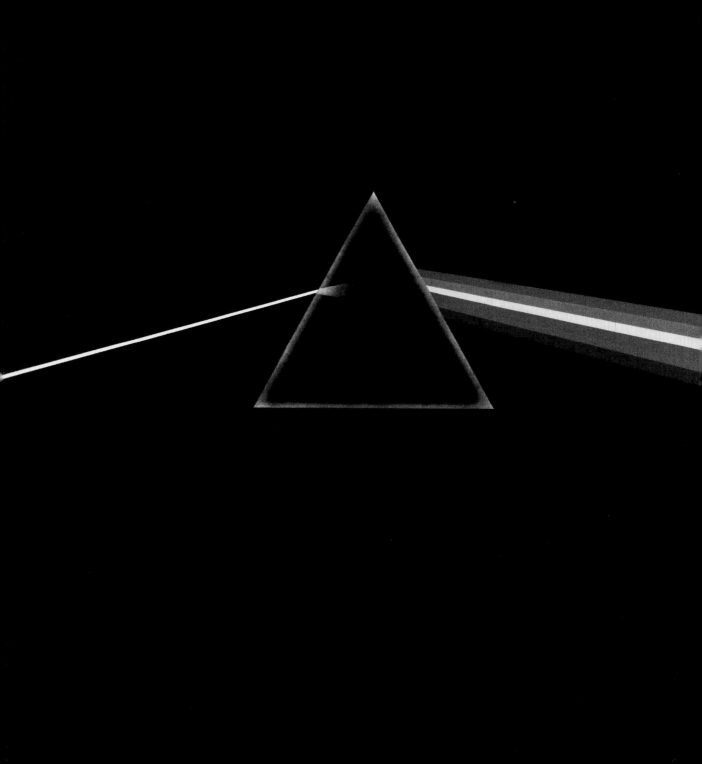

and approachable; the kind of evasive combination that a great many ambitious rock groups had tried, but never quite pulled off.

"I'm not sure we were there for the final mixing of the record at all," says Roger Waters. "It seems weird now; I can't imagine *not* being involved. I think it was just to do with tiredness. Or maybe Dave and I were already starting to fight over things, and it was down to a third party to smooth it all out. And Chris Thomas did smooth it out; he made a very smooth-sounding record. Was I happy with that? Yeah. I remember hearing it and thinking, 'Christ, that sounds really good.'" Gilmour, by contrast, has claimed to have been a little more appreciative: "I can clearly remember that moment: sitting, listening to the whole mix all the *way* through, thinking, 'My God—we've really done something fantastic.'"

Waters arranged for a copy of the final mix to be copied onto his own tape reel, which he took home to North London. "My strongest memory of listening to it," he says, "is when I played it to Judy, who was then my wife. She listened to it all the way through, and when it had finished, she burst into tears. She was very moved by it. I thought, 'That's a very good sign. We've definitely got something here.'"

6

AND WHEN AT LAST THE WORK IS DONE:
THE DARK SIDE OF THE MOON TAKES OFF

Though Roger Waters had intended *The Dark Side of the Moon* to uncouple Pink Floyd from the clichés that had dogged it since the departure of Syd Barrett—psychedelia, science fiction, "space-rock"—it seemed that the group's record company had not quite got the message. Presumably thanks to its title, the album was launched in the group's home country with an opulent party at the London Planetarium—a dome-shaped tourist attraction in which visitors could marvel at a sparkling mock-up of the cosmos before being encouraged to commemorate their visit by buying a selection of astral novelties. Cocktails were served at eight o'clock, followed by a playback of the record "beneath the stars," and "dinner, drinks, and amusements in the arcade." By way of displaying the Floyd's annoyance at the event, Rick Wright was the only member of the band who showed up.

Among the droves of people who took their seats for the premiere was one Roy Hollingworth, a reporter from the weekly *Melody Maker*. Just over a year before, the same paper had bafflingly surmised that the early model of *Dark Side* amounted to a "space fantasy opera"; that night, its empathy

with the band's new creation hardly seemed to have increased. "Ten minutes from blast-off, the music became so utterly confused with itself that it
was virtually impossible to follow," wrote Hollingworth, presumably referring to the transition from "On the Run" to the booming opening of
"Time." "It was becoming less and less attractive, and after fifteen minutes,
decidedly uninteresting." By the time of "The Great Gig in the Sky," he
was apparently not the only one who had all but lost interest. "Quite a few
people were beginning to chatter, and light cigarettes," he went on. "They
looked slightly bored. They had every right to be."

It was only toward the album's close that Hollingworth had begun to
feel any kind of connection with what he heard. "One song in particular
was extremely Syd Barrettsian, to the point of being a straight lift from any
of The Lost Hero's songs," he said, making reference to "a well-spoken
voice, well-echoed, and sad, with wonderfully obvious rhyming to the
lyrics." His account—devoid of song titles, for some reason—suggests that
he may have been referring to either "Us and Them" or "Brain Damage";
if it was the latter, his implied deciphering of the song's subject matter
suggested a sudden attack of true critical brilliance. "Barrett still exists,"
he concluded, "and it was pleasing that the best track on this album is
80 percent–plus influenced by him. And I'll back that up in an argument
with anybody." When the paper ran a full review of the album, they offered
the rather quixotic opinion that *Dark Side* was "perhaps the best Pink
Floyd album since *Ummagumma*."

The *New Musical Express,* mercifully, proved to be a little more percep-
tive. "Musically, this album is not unsimilar to the style formatted with
Atom Heart Mother and *Meddle,"* said the rather stiff review, "though thematically it's stronger, on the most worldly of subjects—madness." Over
the next few weeks, the staff of the paper ratcheted up their enthusiasm,
resulting in an extended salute to the group that appeared a month after
Dark Side's release. "They have emerged from their psychedelic past showing wisdom, maturity, and consistency," said the *NME.* Many of their

readers seemed to be of the same opinion: in its first week on the British chart, *Dark Side* crash-landed in the British album chart at number 4, sitting in between Slade's *Slayed?* and *Billion Dollar Babies* by Alice Cooper.

In the United States, meanwhile, early reports suggested that the album was perfectly placed for the kind of success that its authors had so far missed. In the view of *Billboard, Dark Side* was "a tour de force for lyricist Roger Waters." It went on: "The band is ingrained in a program of heavy, introspective statements, balanced well by their broadly intensive playing. This is music for intense listening." By way of a soundbite for those store owners who required instant enlightenment, *Billboard* advised that *Dark Side* was "avant-garde rock by one of England's most adventurous bands."

Rolling Stone, for some reason, did not get around to dealing with *The Dark Side of the Moon* until May. A 400-word review was squeezed in between a Lester Bangs treatment of *The Best of Bread* ("They got plenty of sex in their songs … don't let nobody tell you they're puds"), and a rather noncommittal treatise on Jefferson Airplane's *Thirty Seconds over Winterland* ("a pretty good rock 'n' roll album"). The *Dark Side* review was written by one Loyd Grossman,[8] a twenty-two-year-old native of Boston, whose prose style was a little more upright than the magazine's countercultural reputation might have suggested—and though he evidently thought highly of the album, hindsight makes at least some of his thoughts seem slightly bizarre.

"It seems to deal primarily with the fleetingness and depravity of human life, hardly the commonplace subject matter of rock," he mused. "'Time,' 'Money,' and 'Us and Them' might be viewed as the keys to understanding the meaning (if indeed there is any definite meaning) of *The Dark Side of the Moon*.… Even though this is a concept album, a number of cuts can stand on their own. 'Time' is a fine country-tinged rocker with a powerful guitar solo by David Gilmour.… the non-vocal 'On the Run' is a standout.… The sound is lush and multi-layered while remaining clear and well-structured.… There are a few weak spots. Gilmour's vocals are

---

[8] Grossman later relocated to the U.K., where he has long been a TV personality specializing in gastronomy. In 1995, he launched his own range of cooking products, based around an array of Indian, Asian, and pasta sauces.

sometimes weak and lackluster and 'The Great Gig in the Sky' could probably have been shortened or dispensed with. But these are quibbles.... There is a certain grandeur here that exceeds mere musical melodramatics and is rarely attempted in rock. *The Dark Side of the Moon* has flash—the true flash that comes from the excellence of a superb performance."

Any musician would surely have been thrilled by such a tribute—but by then, the chatter of music critics had receded into the distance. In the summer of 1973, the success of *The Dark Side of the Moon* was being expressed in an altogether more exciting vocabulary: that of sell-out shows, gold records, and dollars and cents.

Having been released in the United States on March 10, *The Dark Side of the Moon* entered the *Billboard* album chart at the rather underwhelming position of number 95. It was soon gliding upwards, however, sped on its way by a U.S. tour whose timing spoke volumes about Pink Floyd's belief that a breakthrough was imminent. They had begun on March 4 at the Dane County Memorial Coliseum in Madison, Wisconsin; by the time they played the tour's closing date at the Bayfront Center in St. Petersburg, Florida, the album had climbed to 42. And on it went: from 7, to 9, to 6, to 3—and on April 28, to the top position, one place higher than a huge-selling live album entitled *Aloha from Hawaii.* The implication would have brought a shiver of amazement to any young Englishman who had first reached for a guitar in the early days of rock 'n' roll: that week, Pink Floyd really was bigger than Elvis.

The shows that partly propelled *Dark Side* to such a dizzying place were a good deal more ambitious than anything the band had staged before. In addition to Gilmour, Mason, Waters, and Wright, the music was augmented by the presence of three female backing vocalists—two of whom, Carlena Williams and Vanetta Fields, subsequently named themselves the Blackberries—and Dick Parry, co-opted into the touring party to reprise his sax parts on "Money" and "Us and Them." The sound system was a quadraphonic setup of an unprecedented size, and the operation of effects tapes was rehearsed and drilled as never before. The visual elements of the show, meanwhile, were delivered on a scale that would once have been unimaginable: the climax of "On the Run," for example, saw a replica airplane zooming down a set of parallel wires and apparently crashing into the stage.

If all this occasionally seemed to teeter on the brink of overkill, the spectacular nature of the new show could certainly throw the group's human frailties into sharp relief. A soundboard tape from their March 15 show at the Spectrum in Philadelphia attests to the band's largely masterful grasp of their new music, though it's also notable for one or two obvious shortcomings, particularly Waters's occasionally clunky bass playing, and Rick Wright's vocals in the middle sections of "Time." Searchlights doubtless streaked the auditorium, while images of clocks flashed on to the stage, and the backing vocalists added their luxuriant vocal contribution; in the midst of it all, however, he was woefully flat.

Naturally enough, these were trifling concerns. *Dark Side* was selling more and more, and even more auspicious achievements were about to materialize. Much of this, of course, was bound up with the music, and the spectacular impact of the band's live shows—but a great deal of the album's initial momentum could also be traced to the concerted efforts of its American record company.

At the time of the album's U.S. release on Capitol, the newly appointed chairman of the company was Bhaskar Menon, an Indian émigré and Oxford University graduate. Having worked in London as the managing director of EMI's International Division, he had been dispatched to Los Angeles to take up his new job and hack through the problems that were bedeviling EMI's American wing. The company was losing money, chiefly on account of its burdensome roster of artists: in Menon's recollection, he quickly cut down the label's number of acts from around 400 to 83.

Menon's urbane exterior was of a piece with the gentlemanly codes of the more old-school aspects of the English music industry—even now, he refers to the four members of Pink Floyd as "the boys"—but he also conducted his affairs with a single-minded drive. In keeping with all that, he set about attempting to avenge the commercial underachievement that had characterized American sales of Pink Floyd's albums, up to and including

Capitol Records Chairman Bhaskar Menon and Pink Floyd, 1972. "When I saw them play [*Dark Side*], I had the feeling it was like watching one of the great Verdi operas for the first time." (Courtesy of Bhaskar Menon)

Meddle. "It was my firm opinion that those records had underachieved," he says. "There was no question about that: it was obvious. Here were these cutting-edge recording artists, and there seemed to be no reason why the United States was not ready for them. It was difficult to know why things had not gone their way—inappropriate marketing, matters of timing—but I was absolutely determined to make things work."

There was only one problem. By late 1972, Pink Floyd—and, crucially, Steve O'Rourke—were sufficiently disenchanted with Capitol's work on their behalf that they had all but closed a new deal with Columbia, having been charmed by the CBS president, Clive Davis. Some accounts of the band's history couch the move in terms of underhand secrecy ("Capitol was effectively kept in the dark about the Floyd's plans," says one). Bhaskar Menon, however, claims that he was notified of the band's decision well before the end of 1972, whereupon he commenced negotiations aimed at ensuring that the album on which they were working—the last they were obliged to release before formally signing the new contract—would remain Capitol's property. Menon was buoyed by the quiet U.S. success of *Obscured by Clouds*, a record whose momentum had arisen from his insistence that Capitol should quickly make the band a priority.

The crunch conversation came in November 1972, when Menon flew to Marseilles to speak to the group in between their performances with Roland Petit's ballet company. "Nothing could be done about the CBS deal," he says. "But I also had conversations with Steve O'Rourke about giving up *Dark Side*—and I think he probably expected me to say, 'Well, on what terms?' But there were three things that made me determined to work on the record. The first was that it was a kind of test of Capitol's credibility, to see if the company could make it a success. The second was to do with the fact that I admired the music so much. And thirdly, this record was our *due*. In business terms, it was not my practice to voluntarily abandon assets which our shareholders had—like one more Pink Floyd album."

Menon's enthusiasm for *Dark Side*—shared by his colleagues in Los Angeles—had been galvanized by witnessing the American live shows that the band had performed in the spring and fall of 1972. "It was absolutely unique: it struck me as a record that would be as crucial as *Sgt. Pepper,*" he says, emphatically. "The fact that they had played this music in concert was very important: I, and a lot of the people who worked at Capitol, knew about it long before the record came out. And the sheer spectacle of its presentation made it incredible. When I saw them play in 1972, I had the feeling it was like watching one of the great Verdi operas for the first time. It had that kind of impact."

As Menon's operatic analogy suggests, his appreciation of the Floyd's new music was founded in something that ran a little deeper than the potential for huge sales; even in his initial exposure to *Dark Side,* he claims to have detected the rough outlines of the album's defining themes. "It was unbelievably *stirring* music," he says. "In the early '70s—after the drug years, and this harsh, committed climate of the late '60s—it had a wonderful sense of intelligence, and sensitivity. And it conveyed an adult kind of disenchantment, but also a concern about the state of the world."

Menon resolved to rapidly build on the enthusiastic press notices and devoted U.S. audience Pink Floyd had slowly amassed through the early 1970s and institute an unprecedented push: "a marketing campaign which was far more extensive than anything the record company had ever done." If the Floyd's modus operandi had occasionally suggested the notion of art for art's sake, the commercial game was now played with enthusiasm—though Menon recalls the group being a little less reticent than their reputation might have suggested. "They were four very private people: not the sort who relished Platinum Record parties," he says. "But we organized a party for the press in New York, in a restaurant, and I asked Steve O'Rourke if the boys would like to come. I wasn't very hopeful that they would. But they did. They were ambitious; they knew the record was a crucial work. Definitely."

As the album collided with the American public, advertisements ("*The Dark Side of the Moon*—a superb number 1 Gold album") blanketed the U.S. press. "Us and Them" and "Time" were edited into new condensed versions, so as to further endear them to radio programmers. Once the ears of DJs had been turned to this new, remarkably FM–compatible sound, the rest was easy. As Alan Parsons later pointed out, "The album was perfect fodder for American radio. It was very programmable. If a jock wanted to play two or three tracks, one after the other, he'd had his work done for him, because all the segues were carefully worked out within the grooves."

The results of all this were soon evident in the band's ascent to the top of the album chart—but Menon, in cahoots with Steve O'Rourke ("Steve was driven; he had a good mind, but he was never frenetic," he says) had yet more ambitious plans: to break with one of Pink Floyd's tacit rules, and promote *Dark Side* via the release of a single. "It took a considerable amount of persuasion; they needed a lot of convincing," says Menon. "In the first phase of the album, it went to number one, and sold a huge number of records. That was the first part of its career, if you like. What it needed was a catalyst that would quickly propel it on to the next kind of audience. And that meant breaking into AM radio—Top 40 radio—which

(opposite) Earl's Court Arena, London, May 1973. (Jill Furmanovsky)

was playing all kinds of music, none of which were anything like *Dark Side*."

Pink Floyd had not put out a single since the British release of "Point Me at the Sky," a Roger Waters composition that had stiffed at the end of 1968. Now, there was one obvious option, so glaring as to be a no-brainer. So it was that "Money" ("an almost self-evident choice," according to Menon) was recast in a new shortened version, sent to radio stations having been divested of the word "bullshit," and twinned with "Any Colour You Like" as its B-side. It was released on May 12; by June 30, it was sitting at number 26, one place below Tony Orlando and Dawn's saccharine tribute to the troops returning home from Vietnam, "Tie a Yellow Ribbon Round the Old Oak Tree." In the end, it managed to climb another thirteen places.

By then, having returned to the U.K. to play two shows at the 20,000-capacity Earl's Court Arena in London, Pink Floyd was dutifully back in the United States for a twelve-date tour, bookended by two dates that marked their reluctant induction into the world of what came to be known as stadium rock. The trip began with a show at the Roosevelt Stadium in Jersey City, and having taken in a slew of indoor auditoriums, ended at the 74,000-capacity Tampa Stadium. It was now that Pink Floyd bumped into one of the more absurdly circular elements of their new success. Having been gratefully prised off the English ballroom circuit by their post-Barrett acquisition of a high-end, distinctly cerebral kind of audience, they were presented with a new crowd that, once again, simply wanted to hear The Big Hit. In Carlisle, Dunstable, and Aberdeen, they had numbered no more than a couple of hundred; now, Pink Floyd were faced with endless thousands.

"The thing I remember most about the period after that was the incredible annoyance at the gigs," Gilmour later recalled. "We were doing these places where all the young kids would be shouting 'Money!' all the way through the show. We'd been used to all these reverent fans.... We'd try to get really quiet, especially at the beginning of 'Echoes,' and kids would be there shouting, 'Money!'"

"It took me until ten years ago to stop being upset that people whistled through the quiet numbers," said Waters in 1987. "I used to stop and go, 'Right! Who's whistling? Come on—be quiet!'"

"When you get to that size, there's no prayer in hell of everyone being there because they love your music," says Gilmour. "A lot of them are there for the party, and they're not necessarily there because they've bought your record and loved it. They've paid their money, so it's their choice. That was a big change at that time: there were a lot of people who wanted us to do something that we didn't quite want to do. They wanted us to play more uptempo stuff, and they wanted to groove around and dance and shout and drink beer from their coolers and have a good time. We did have to change the things we did a little bit. Did we feel compromised by that? Yes. But what can you do about it? You're kind of stuck."

If the experience of entertaining their newly expanded audiences seemed to be giving the Floyd the feeling that their live shows had now passed out of their control, some of the ideas that were being attached to *The Dark Side of the Moon* must have only served to heighten their sense of powerless-

The Floyd's newly expanded public welcome them back to London's Rainbow, November 1973. Waters later admitted to being "upset that people whistled through the quiet numbers." (Jill Furmanovsky)

(following pages) Gilmour and Waters, making the best of on-tour downtime in 1974. "When you get to that size, there's no prayer in hell of everyone being there because they love your music...." (Jill Furmanovsky)

ness. In the popular consciousness, empathy, insanity, and all the rest of Waters's subject matter proved to be a little less noteworthy than the simple uses to which the record could be put—not least, its widely acclaimed suitability to the bedroom. "I've heard so many people say that they like to shag to it," says David Gilmour. "Phil Everly told me that: that it was his favorite album for having sex to."

There was another commonplace association that soon became irrevocably glued to *Dark Side,* embodied in the idea that it was the "ultimate

stoner album." The fact that Waters's lyrics were so direct and articulate as to lie light-years from the stuff of archetypal weed-rock—and that the band were hardly prodigious cannabis users—mattered little: within the sensurround ambience of "Breathe," "The Great Gig in the Sky," and "Brain Damage," there was surely an ideal soundtrack for those who liked to while away their time in a haze of fragrant smoke.

"Rick and I would have a puff on the occasional joint, but Roger and Nick didn't," says Gilmour. "We weren't making our records under the influence of dope, but we'd come out of what was called the psychedelic era, so none of us were shocked by that kind of stuff. And I do think that our sort of music was more conducive to that sort of thing than many others; we'd been involved in making music for the mind as well as the heart, going back some considerable time. But it wasn't an essential part of us."

"Making love and smoking marijuana are both perfectly reasonable activities in my view," says Roger Waters. "I think you can take smoking marijuana to extremes that aren't very good for you. You can waste an awful lot of time. But I think it's hard to have too much sex."

Dark Side comic (Nick Mason's Archive)

"If I'm honest," says Waters, "I have to accept that at that point, I became a capitalist. You can call yourself what the fuck you like, but if you suddenly get quite a lot of money, the impression is that you're a capitalist. You can't pretend … you can espouse humanitarian ideas, which I still do, but things are that bit more complicated."

Given Waters's lyrics on "Money" ("I'm in the high-fidelity first-class travelling set/And I think I need a Lear jet"), the success of *The Dark Side of the Moon* represented a glaring case of life eventually imitating art. The band's earnings prior to that album had been satisfactory, but by the standards of the '70s rock aristocracy, they were still leading comparatively frugal lifestyles. "Up to *Dark Side,* we didn't have much money," says Nick Mason. "We were always paying back equipment debts. It wasn't until after the album that we all had houses rather than flats."

As 1973 rolled on, however, their bank accounts began to swell, not least on account of their new deal with CBS, which brought them a rumored advance of £1 million. As far as Roger Waters was concerned, the band's ever-increasing wealth was not the cause of unqualified joy: given the beliefs that had been instilled in him throughout his upbringing, he recalls his skyrocketing earnings causing him no little disquiet. "When you suddenly make a lot of money," he says, "you have to decide whether to give it away to poor people or invest it. I decided to give some of it away to poor people and invest the rest.

"I was faced with that dilemma, coming from the background I did. I could no longer pretend that I was a true socialist, but 25 percent of it went into a charitable trust that I've run ever since. I don't make a song and dance about it; it's mainly based in England, and mainly to do with kids. The usual sort of stuff. One of the good things about being a capitalist, is that you become a philanthropist, to a certain extent."

If his words suggest a graceful resolution of the problems presented by his newly acquired fortune, other members of the band have occasionally recalled slightly more awkward episodes. "After *The Dark Side of the Moon*," said Rick Wright in 1994, "we had a bit of money and I bought a house in the country. I had two young children. Roger sat down and said to me, 'I can't believe you've done this—you've sold out, I think it's disgusting.' Six months later, he went and bought a much bigger house in the country. I said, 'Remember what you said?' He said, 'Ah, yes—but that's because my wife wanted it, not me.' Absolute bullshit. I found him rather hypocritical. That's what angered me about him."

For the characteristically upbeat Nick Mason—who would soon become a keen collector of expensive automobiles—there did not seem much to worry about. "The money seemed to come in fairly gradually," he says. "But there was a moment when I thought, 'Oh, I can buy that car.' I bought a 275 GTB Ferrari, because I couldn't quite afford a GTO at the time."

It took Pink Floyd until January 1975 to begin their next album. As with *The Dark Side of the Moon,* new songs had been worked up in rehearsal, and played at a run of live shows—this time, in France and the United Kingdom. Among them was "Shine On You Crazy Diamond," an impassioned hymn to Syd Barrett that found Roger Waters developing some of the themes at which he had hinted in "Brain Damage"—and though that song alone hardly suggested any kind of creative impasse, its promise failed to foster any real sense of momentum. Something had been mislaid: the sense of drive and purpose that had propelled the band from Broadhurst Gardens, through the United States, Japan, and Europe and on to the triumphs that had been put to tape at Abbey Road. In so transforming their universe, success had caused them to question all its aspects: the group, their talents, the bonds that endured—in some cases—since the mid-1960s. Perhaps inevitably, this sense of once-solid certainties being laid waste extended far beyond their working lives; it was this period, for example, that saw the end of Waters's first marriage.

In retrospect, the band may well have come close to splitting up—though given what could be either charitably viewed as English reserve or maligned as an eternal inability to genuinely commune with one another, precious little of their internal friction was ever brought into the open. "It's not that we thought we were about to implode or explode—just talking to people afterwards, everyone seemed to be a bit despondent," says Nick Mason. "Certainly, I couldn't quite see what we were going to do next." Once again, to use his own phrase, "getting started was the problem"; a difficulty surely made worse by the same emotional awkwardness that, back in 1967, had made the decline of Syd Barrett yet more problematic. If *The Dark Side of the Moon* made the case for empathy and understanding, its authors still seemed to have soaked up precious little of its message.

Thus, when they belatedly regrouped at Abbey Road, there was a quiet sense of crisis. "At the *Wish You Were Here* recording sessions," Waters later recalled, "most of us didn't wish we were there at all; we wished we were somewhere else. I wasn't happy being there because I got the feeling we weren't together."

It's perhaps telling that Dave Gilmour—never as innately optimistic as Nick Mason, but not nearly as self-questioning a character as Waters—claims to have arrived at the sessions having passed through the process of picking through who he was and the direction in which his life was moving. "I suppose I gradually came to the conclusion that I was a musician and I did like making music," he says. "But the success did have a distinct effect on the way we all were and a distinct effect on the genesis and creation of *Wish You Were Here*. It's well documented that Roger thought we were very absent during the making of that album, and that no one really wanted to be in the studio, doing it. I suppose we all thought it about everyone but ourselves at that time. But after that feeling of slight emptiness came another great album—just as good in my view, if not better."

Nonetheless, something had changed. In the context of the decade that would elapse before Roger Waters formally called time on his involvement in Pink Floyd, the idea that *The Dark Side of the Moon* represented the beginning of the end might seem rather misplaced. Quite apart from tour schedules that would define much of the next six years, there were three more albums to come—including a climactic record that, in financial terms at least, would outstrip the achievements of *Dark Side*.

Yet in his more heavy-hearted moments, that's precisely the picture painted by the stridently ambitious figure who had piloted the band to a point so dizzying that they were faced with no option but to gradually come down. "*The Dark Side of the Moon* finished off Pink Floyd once and for all," Roger Waters once reflected. "To be that successful is the aim of every group. And once you've cracked it, it's all over."

APPENDIX
US AND THEM: LIFE AFTER *THE DARK SIDE OF THE MOON*

David Gilmour remained a working member of Pink Floyd for twenty-one years after the release of *The Dark Side of the Moon,* though that period saw two lengthy breaks: from 1983 to 1986, as Roger Waters's role within the band drew to a close and Gilmour finally launched the third incarnation of the group; and from 1989 to 1993, from the end of touring around *A Momentary Lapse of Reason* to the start of work on *The Division Bell.* After the Floyd were put on indefinite hold in 1994, Gilmour kept a low profile, making the odd guest appearance—he contributed, for example, to Paul McCartney's 1999 covers album *Run Devil Run*—but deciding not to add to a small solo catalogue whose last entry was *About Face,* released in 1984. His last commercial release was a DVD entitled *David Gilmour in Concert,* released in 2002, on which he performed such Pink Floyd songs as "Shine On You Crazy Diamond," "Comfortably Numb," and "Fat Old Sun," the Syd Barrett original "Terrapin," and "Hushabye Mountain" from the movie *Chitty Chitty Bang Bang.* Against not inconsiderable odds, he announced in the summer of 2005 that he would reunite with Roger Waters for Pink

Floyd's appearance at Live 8.

Nick Mason maintained his role as Pink Floyd's drummer until 1994, though the success of *The Dark Side of the Moon* had allowed him to pursue an interest in motor sport that eventually took precedence over his musical activities. He rekindled his friendship with Roger Waters after an accidental meeting in the summer of 2002, in the wake of which he made a guest appearance at a Waters solo show in London, adding drums to a rendition of "Set the Controls for the Heart of the Sun." He published *Inside Out: A Personal History of Pink Floyd,* in September 2004. While promoting the book, he was asked about the chances of a Pink Floyd reunion including Gilmour and Waters. "The only way it would happen," he said, "would be another thing like Live Aid, where you'd say, 'This is more important than any differences, and we'll do something wonderful.' It's not logically impossible. But you'd have to talk to the others. I've always been an optimist." Less than a year later, his hopes were realized when the four members of Pink Floyd Mk II agreed to appear together at Live 8.

Roger Waters served notice of the end of Pink Floyd in October 1986, with a legal suit claiming that the band "should be allowed to retire gracefully." Much to his annoyance, David Gilmour then revived the band—"I'm not sure how they're going to manage, considering I was the only one who would ever do anything for about the last fifteen years," he said—leaving Waters to pursue the solo career that had begun with *The Pros and Cons of Hitchhiking* (1984). It also resulted in *Radio K.A.O.S.* (1987), *Amused to Death* (1992), and a live album entitled *In the Flesh* (2000). In 1990, he staged an all-star production of *The Wall* in Berlin, aimed at making money for the Memorial Fund for Disaster Relief, a charity pledged to raise five English pounds for every life lost in the wars of the twentieth century. At the time of writing, he was involved in two projects that had been ongoing for several years: an opera centered on the French revolution entitled *Ça Ira*

("We'll Make It") and a Broadway version of *The Wall*. "I don't think there should necessarily be a separation from the records I made with Pink Floyd and the work I've done since," he says. "That's the voice that ran through those years, and that voice has continued." Waters's agreement to rejoin Gilmour, Mason, and Rick Wright at Live 8 was couched in terms of a temporary reunion: A statement released to the press talked of an opportunity "to put the band back together, even if it's only for a few numbers."

Rick Wright was perhaps the most evident casualty of Roger Waters's increasing dominance of Pink Floyd. "When he started developing his ego trips," Wright later claimed, "the person he would have his conflicts with would be me." Though Waters dismissed him from the band during the recording of *The Wall*, Wright was paid a wage to return for the project's concert performances. In a similarly semi-detached capacity, he played keyboards with Gilmour's incarnation of Pink Floyd, until being reinstated as full member prior to the recording of *The Division Bell*. He released his second solo album, *Broken China*, in 1996—and has since quietly entered a period of effective retirement, broken only by Pink Floyd's appearance at Live 8. In the eyes of some of the group's associates, his contribution to the band has long been overlooked; in the view of Peter Jenner, for example, Wright "is the great unsung hero of the Floyd."

Syd Barrett lives in Cambridge. In the wake of his departure from Pink Floyd, he recorded two albums—*The Madcap Laughs* and *Barrett*—partly assisted by Roger Waters, David Gilmour, and Rick Wright, before his musical activities became sporadic and eventually ended. His last meeting with all three of his ex-colleagues took place in June 1975, when he unexpectedly paid a visit to Abbey Road during the recording of *Wish You Were Here*, and his physical appearance alone—in Nick Mason's memoirs, he is described as "a large fat bloke with a shaven head, wearing a decrepit old tan mac"—caused them no little dismay. "I didn't have a *clue* who he was," says Mason. "I can recall someone saying, 'Do you know who this is, Nick?' And me staring, thinking, 'Well … no.'" These days, though music apparently plays no role in his life, Barrett is said to be a keen amateur painter. "Syd's never been short of cash, from his work," says Roger Waters. "His publishing money is still quite considerable. And he has fairly simple tastes. He doesn't live in a castle. He has his own house, and he potters about."

Lesley Duncan ceased her work as a session singer not long after *The Dark Side of the Moon,* and released a number of her own albums. She quit the music business in the 1980s, and now lives in the Scottish Hebrides.

Peter Jenner followed his time with Pink Floyd with a successful career in management: his clients have included Tyrannosaurus Rex, Roy Harper, Kevin Ayers, the Clash, Ian Dury & the Blockheads, the Disposable Heroes of Hiphoprisy, and the English singer-songwriter Billy Bragg. He is currently chairman of the International Music Managers' Forum.

John Leckie graduated from being one of Abbey Road's staff engineers to a successful career as a producer. His credits include XTC's *White Music,* Radiohead's 1995 album *The Bends,* the self-titled debut by the Stone Roses, and, more recently, the first two albums by the British trio Muse.

Bhaskar Menon remained chairman of Capitol until 1978, when he was appointed chairman of EMI Worldwide. He left the EMI organization in 1990, and still lives in Los Angeles. Looking back at his role in *The Dark Side of the Moon,* he says, "I had always believed that the record would be very, very successful. It was gratifying—but not surprising."

Steve O'Rourke remained Pink Floyd's manager until his death in October 2003. At his funeral service at Chichester Cathedral, England, Gilmour,

Wright, and Mason played the Pink Floyd songs "Fat Old Sun" and "The Great Gig in the Sky."

Dick Parry was a fixture of Pink Floyd's live shows until the close of touring that accompanied 1977's *Animals.* After a break from professional musicianship, he played on *The Division Bell,* and joined the assembly of musicians who assisted David Gilmour, Nick Mason, and Rick Wright on the World Tour that followed its release. In 2004, he played a run of shows with the cultish U.S. indie-rock band the Violent Femmes.

Alan Parsons founded his own musical enterprise the Alan Parsons Project in 1976; its first album was *Tales of Mystery and Imagination,* a conceptual work inspired by the writings of Edgar Allan Poe. The enterprise lasted until the mid-1990s, when Parsons launched the solo career that led to a 2004 album entitled *A Valid Path,* which featured contributions from David Gilmour. When *The Dark Side of the Moon* was remixed in 5.1 surround sound, Parsons expressed his hurt at not being invited to do the job himself. "It was already underway when I found out," he said. "I was very angry." Though Roger Waters and David Gilmour have occasionally sought to play down Parsons's contribution to *Dark Side,* at least one member of Pink Floyd is fulsome in his praise. "I think he was particularly responsible for the sonic perfection of the record," says Nick Mason. "For the period, it was astonishingly good."

Aubrey Powell continued his association with Pink Floyd until *Animals,* called time on his involvement in sleeve design in the 1980s, and is now a filmmaker. He has made documentaries about the English artist Francis Bacon and the Zulu and Xhosa tribes of South Africa, as well as making occasional forays into TV advertising.

Barry St. John continued her work as a vocalist until the early 1980s, before concluding that "session singing doesn't go on forever." After training at night school, she entered the legal profession, in which she still works.

Liza Strike numbers among the most-recorded rock backing vocalists ever: by her own estimate, she has appeared on over eighty different albums. After her role on *Dark Side,* she continued her career as a session singer, until a spell of illness in the early 1980s. She then moved from London to the English coastal town of Plymouth, where she has worked as a singing teacher. As with most of *Dark Side's* supporting cast, she did not receive a complimentary copy of the album. Three years after its release, however, she had a chance social meeting with Dave Gilmour. "I said to him, 'Hey, Dave—have you got a copy of the record?' Like you do when you're young and loose." Gilmour could not oblige; instead, he handed her a copy of *Wish You Were Here.*

Chris Thomas has long been among rock music's most admired producers. He followed his work on *The Dark Side of the Moon* with the cementing of his production role with Roxy Music, followed in turn by his work on *Never Mind the Bollocks, Here's the Sex Pistols.* His other credits include the first three albums by the Pretenders, INXS's *Kick* and *Different Class,* and *This Is Hardcore* by the English band Pulp. He recently worked with U2 on their 2004 album *How to Dismantle an Atomic Bomb.*

Storm Thorgeson worked with Pink Floyd on the artwork for *Wish You Were Here* and *Animals,* but was not used for *The Wall.* He resumed his association from 1987's *A Momentary Lapse of Reason* onwards, and his designs have graced such recent projects as *The Dark Side of the Moon's* 30th Anniversary reissue, a DVD of *Live at Pompeii,* and Nick Mason's book *Inside Out.* The third edition of his own book, *Mind over Matter,* appeared in 2003.

Clare Torry discovered by chance that the vocal part she recorded for "The Great Gig in the Sky" had been included on *The Dark Side of the Moon.* "I was walking past a record shop," she says, "and in the window was a huge poster of the prism and spectrum of light, and I saw the words 'Pink Floyd' and thought, 'I wonder if that's the album I did that singing on.' I bought it and took it back home, and played it from the beginning. And I thought it was fantastic." During the 1970s, her work was split between TV commercials and sessions with the likes of Meat Loaf, Olivia Newton-John, and Tangerine Dream. In the late 1980s, with Rick Wright's blessing, she re-recorded "The Great Gig in the Sky" for a British painkillers ad; her link with Pink Floyd was also revived via an appearance on Roger Waters's 1987 album *Radio K.A.O.S* and a rendition of "The Great Gig in the Sky" at a huge outdoor Floyd show at Knebworth Park, Hertfordshire, in June 1990. After retiring from professional work, Torry pursued a claim to songwriting royalties from *The Dark Side of the Moon,* on account of her melodic contribution to "The Great Gig in the Sky." "At first," she says, "the costs were prohibitively expensive. I had to swallow it, really. And also, if I'd started something when I was well into my career, I'd have been thought of as a troublemaker. So once I'd retired, I thought about it again. It went on from there." The case was settled in Torry's favor in the spring of 2005. She is prohibited from releasing any information about the out-of-court agreement, aside from the fact that the song will now be credited to "Wright/Torry."

Doris Troy continued her work as a British-based solo performer and session singer before returning to the United States in the late 1970s, where she became involved with *Mama, I Want to Sing,* a musical based on her life, which subsequently became one of the most successful off-Broadway shows in history. She died on February 16, 2004, in Las Vegas.

Bibliography/Sources

This book is based on interviews by the author with David Gilmour, Nick Mason, Roger Waters, Alan Parsons, Clare Torry, Lesley Duncan, Liza Strike, Barry St. John, John Leckie, Peter Jenner, Bhaskar Menon, and Aubrey Powell.

It would also have been nothing without the mountain of accomplished scholarship on which any writing about Pink Floyd inevitably draws. My biggest debts here are to *Pink Floyd: In the Flesh* by Glenn Povey and Ian Russell (Bloomsbury, 1997), the definitive and wonderfully presented guide to the band's live career, which is recommended without qualification; and Vernon Fitch's *Pink Floyd: The Press Reports* (Collectors Guide Publishing, 2001), an unbelievably thorough dossier that illuminated my path through the archives of the British Library. The following works also proved invaluable:

David Cooper (ed.), *The Dialectics of Liberation* (Pelican, 1968)

Jonathan Green, *Days in the Life: Voices from the English Underground 1961–1971* (Pimlico, 1988)

Nick Hodges and Ian Priston, *Embryo: A Pink Floyd Chronology* (Cherry Red Books, 1999)

R. D. Laing, *The Politics of Experience/The Bird of Paradise* (Penguin, 1967) and *Self and Others* (Pelican, 1971)

Andy Mabbett, *The Complete Guide to the Music of Pink Floyd* (Omnibus Press, 1995)

Miles and Andy Mabbett, *Pink Floyd: The Visual Documentary* (Omnibus Press, 1994)

Nick Mason, *Inside Out: A Personal History of Pink Floyd* (Weidenfield & Nicolson, 2004)

David Parker, *Random Precision: Recording the Music of Syd Barrett 1965–1974* (Cherry Red Books, 2001)

Nicholas Schaffner, *Saucerful of Secrets: The Pink Floyd Odyssey* (Helter Skelter, 2003)

Brian Southall, Peter Vince, and Allan Rouse, *Abbey Road* (Omnibus Press, 2002)

M. C. Strong, *The Wee Rock Discography* (Canongate, 1996)

Storm Thorgeson, *Mind over Matter: The Images of Pink Floyd* (Sanctuary, 2003)

Mike Watkinson and Pete Anderson, *Crazy Diamond: Syd Barrett & the Dawn of Pink Floyd* (Omnibus Press, 1991)

Tim Willis, *Madcap: The Half-Life of Syd Barrett, Pink Floyd's Lost Genius* (Short Books, 2003)

Periodicals, websites, and other sources

My biggest thanks on this score go to two people: the great Matt Johns, who graciously answered my requests for Floyd-related information, and—far more importantly—runs the brilliant website at www.brain-damage.co.uk; and Mark Blake, editor of the superlative *Q/Mojo* Pink Floyd special published in 2004.

Three definitive British magazine articles proved extremely instructive and are recommended without hesitation to any student of Pink Floyd's history: "Lost in Space" by Carol Clerk, published in *Uncut* 73 (June 2003); Phil Sutcliffe and Peter Henderson's "The First Men on the Moon," from *Mojo* 67 (July 1999); and Johnny Black's "The Long March," published in *Mojo* 96 (November 2001). In addition to *Q, Mojo,* and *Uncut,* the text also draws on past issues of *Melody Maker, NME, Disc & Music Echo, Sounds, Rolling Stone, The Guardian, Vancouver Free Press, Zig Zag,* and *Billboard.*

On the Internet, I also found admirable stores of information at Jakub Crawford's Pink Floyd Hyperbase (http://pinkfloydhyperbase.dk) and Vernon Fitch's Pink Floyd Archives (http://ourworld.compuserve.com/homepages/PFArchives).

Perhaps most importantly, I could not have done without two DVDs that shine crucial light on this period of Pink Floyd's history. *Classic Albums: The Making of The Dark Side of the Moon* (Eagle Vision, 2003) represents the acme of the musical documentary-maker's art, and I owe special thanks to its co-producer Martin R. Smith, for vital help with contacts. Adrian Maben's *Live at Pompeii: The Director's Cut* (Universal, 2002) is also highly recommended, both as an encapsulation of its era and as a gracefully executed look at the band circa 1971–73.

Acknowledgments

Massive thanks go to Ben Schafer at Da Capo Press, a great editor, sounding board, and Floyd expert whose patience, graciousness, and expertise merit a heartfelt salute. I am also grateful to Jason Fine at *Rolling Stone,* whose commission of a *Dark Side* article in January 2003 was the seed from which this book sprang; my U.S. agent, Sarah Lazin, and Hannah Griffiths, whose initial input got things on the right track; and Nick Davies, ex of Fourth Estate and now at Hodder. Awestruck thanks go to Storm Thorgeson for his design of the cover—and I'm particularly indebted to Emily Hedges for the brilliant picture research that took the book into a completely different dimension.

Thanks also to the following: Ian Russell for so generously contributing archive posters and tickets; Ian Harrison at *Mojo* and Merope Mills at *The Guardian,* for two fantastically useful commissions; the staff of *Q* and *Mojo,* for their hospitality and help with back issues; Tom Sutherland of Tom's records of Hay on Wye (www.tomsrecords.com); Marina Rendle; Kay Garner; Andy Mabbett, Allan Rouse, my Mum and Dad; Phyl and Paul Mighall; Karl Rhys, whose warnings about elephants were timely but mercifully ill-founded; and Steve Lowe. Huge gratitude, as ever, goes to Hywel Harris, for his friendship, inspiration, and inestimable web design, of which I am only one of many beneficiaries (for details, visit www.hywel.biz).

My greatest appreciation, however, is for Ginny Luckhurst, to whose love, grace, and patience words don't really do justice.

—John Harris, Hay on Wye, March 2005

Index

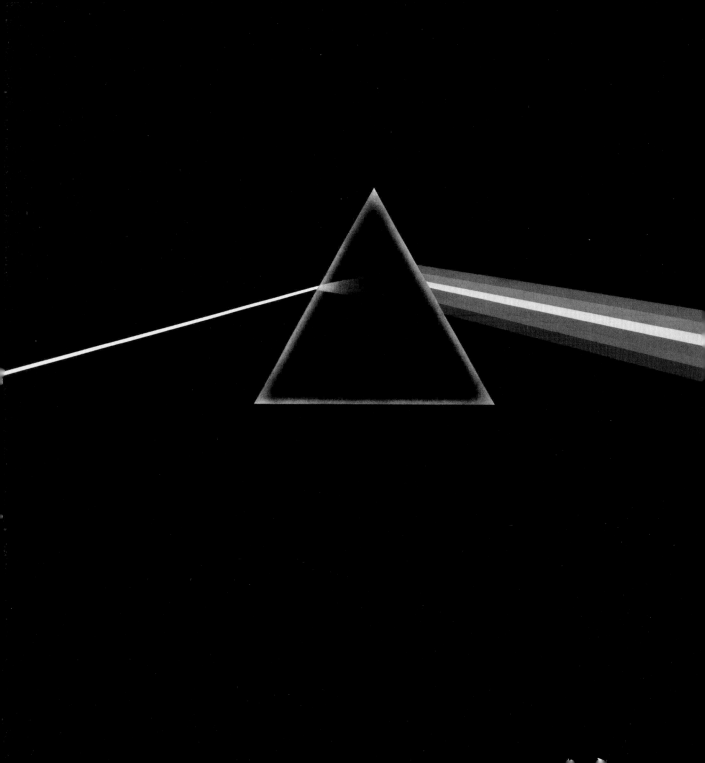